D1346477

RADICAL REJUVENATION

Roxy Dillon has a BSc in Psychology from Bristol University and an MSc in Biochemical Pharmacology from Southampton University. She has studied at the Institute of Neurology and at University College London. For the past fifteen years she has worked as a nutritionist, herbalist and aromatherapist.

At the age of thirty-six she decided to stop crying every time she saw herself in the mirror and to do something about it instead. She put all her past knowledge and experience (plus!) to work on the problem and Radical Rejuvenation was born.

Roxy Dillon lives in East Anglia with her husband, three children and many animals.

'*Radical Rejuvenation* is a fascinating book that will yield special benefits to anyone who follows it. Roxy Dillon has combined a tremendous amount of research and personal experience which gives a significant authority to this book.'

Gabriel Cousens, MD, holistic physician and author of *Conscious Eating*

'Impressive and remarkable ... obviously the culmination of a massive amount of reading and personal research. The book warrants careful study and repeated readings.'

Robert L. Erdmann, PhD, author of *The Amino Revolution*

RADICAL REJUVENATION

The Revolutionary New System for
Reversing the Effects of Ageing

Roxy Dillon

HEADLINE

First published in 1996
by HEADLINE BOOK PUBLISHING

10 9 8 7 6 5 4 3 2 1

ISBN 0 7472 5194 0

Typeset by Keyboard Services, Luton, Beds

Printed and bound in Great Britain by
Cox & Wyman Ltd, Reading, Berks

HEADLINE BOOK PUBLISHING
A division of Hodder Headline PLC
338 Euston Road
London NW1 3BH

To my husband and children.

This book is also for my parents and for Standa
and Anka.

This book is not intended to take the place of medical advice. If you are suffering from a medical condition, or if you are pregnant, considering a pregnancy and not using an effective means of contraception, or if you are breast feeding, do not follow any advice given in this book without prior consultation with a nutritionist, aromatherapist, herbalist or GP. The suggestions given in this book *cannot* be applied to young children and infants.

Contents

Acknowledgements

Thanks to my agent, Serafina Clarke, and her very gifted assistant, Amanda White, for their enthusiasm and editorial help; to Lorraine Jerram (especially for being there on the phone – you know why) for being a fine, imaginative editor; and to Alan Brooke.

Thanks also to Dr Robert Erdmann, Dr Gabriel Cousens and Dr Sarah Brewer for reading the manuscript.

I have been inspired and aided by the work of many original thinkers in the field of nutrition, herbalism and raw food therapy. Most notably, I would like to acknowledge my debt to the following researchers: Leslie Kenton, Dr Robert Erdmann, Dr Gabriel Cousens, Michael Murray, Michael Tierra, Dr Vasant Lad, David Frawley, Dr S. Dharmananda, James Green, Ann Wigmore, Viktoras Kulvinskas, Sheila Andrews, Morris Krok, Dr Mervyn Werbach, Daniel Reid, Joseph E. Pizzorno, Dr Daniel Mowrey, Dr Sheldon Saul Hendler, Leon Chaitow, Ron Teeguarden, Dr Max Bircher-Benner, Dr Edmund Szekely, Hilton Hotema, David Klein, Joe Alexander, Marcia Acciardo, Dr Stephen Davies, Dr Alan Stewart, Dr H. L. Newbold, Rudolph Ballantine, Dr Leon Gallard, Jean Carper, Dr Edward Howell, Durk Pearson, Sandy Shaw, Dr James Devlin, Dr O. L. M. Abramowski, T. C. Fry and Dick Gregory.

I mention them with the understanding that their expertise has furthered my knowledge but that this book reflects my beliefs, not necessarily theirs.

Foreword

This book is not for scientists. It's for people whose bodies flag and sag and bag and droop, whose expression lines stay long after the expressions have gone, who see someone much older than themselves when they look in the mirror. And who aren't yet resigned to it all.

This book describes a programme called Radical Rejuvenation which produces visible results and can reverse already existing effects of ageing. It consists of external and internal methods and includes a diet, advice on herbs, nutritional supplements, including amino acids, enzymes and oils for internal use and similar factors for external application.

Here you will find reasons why you don't have to accept wrinkles, fat and other signs of ageing as inevitable. And suggestions to reverse and avoid such changes.

In the first part of the book you will learn what is possible. In the second part you will learn some interesting reasons for the suggested remedies. Since some products will not be familiar to you, you will also find explanations on nutritional supplements (and the best brands available), herbs (where to buy them and how to take them) and the few gadgets which you need, such as a blender and a juicer. At the end of the book there is information on where to obtain the products mentioned, including mail order companies, so that you can benefit equally whether you live near Piccadilly Circus or in the Outer Hebrides.

There are also outlines for effective rejuvenation programmes. In Part Three you will find detailed instructions for the Basic, Intermediate, Gold Band and Cheat's programmes. The Basic is for those who'd like to try some of the suggestions in this book without going all the way. The Intermediate programme is for those who would like to see faster results, while the Gold Band is for desperados – and aren't we all after thirty-five! And the Cheat's programme is for those who want to look better than they have for years without avoiding those occasional treats in life.

The other day my ten-year-old daughter turned to me and said, 'You're the prettiest mum in the world.' I know that opinion may be somewhat divided on this. Never mind. But the point is, it wasn't just blind love talking because she followed it up with, 'I'm not ashamed to be seen with you any more.' So maybe she won't make a great politician but at least she was kind enough not to tell me way back then. It turns out, way back then she thought I looked dumpy, drab and dull. And OLD. But I turned it around. I did it without make-up, surgery or trips to the hairdresser. I look good now. I look the way I want to look. I look like me and I like it. That's a first for me.

I like the way I look because it's healthy and young and honest. The youthfulness is part of it all – super health is young. Radical Rejuvenation is young.

There is too much depression around. They'll tell you it can't be done. Don't listen to them. Ageing is far less connected with your actual age than they say. Ageing is connected with your biochemistry. And you can have a great impact on that. You can improve your biochemical age. And it will show, I promise you.

You can affect the rate at which you age. This book will show you how.

PART ONE

What Radical Rejuvenation Can Do for You

The Programme

I don't believe in ageing. I tried it and I didn't like it. I tried wrinkles and awful hair, flabby arms and a sex drive that would make a eunuch sing. I tried looking my age, I even tried looking my mother's age. It doesn't have a lot going for it. So I put together a radical programme for rejuvenation which actually works – producing visible, fast improvements in looks and vitality so that I (and anyone else who follows it) never have to 'look my age' again. I have called it Radical Rejuvenation (RR) because the improvements this programme brings are radical and the programme itself, of course, is also radical. Let's face it, if there was any vitality to be found in the normal Western fare of chocolate, cream and cheese, there'd be an awful lot of stunners around – which there aren't. Most of us feel bad and are getting worse most of the time. As for looks – even the few lucky ones who manage to limp on till thirty-five begin to panic soon after that.

Cosmetic surgery is not radical. It's extreme, but not radical. It's no good having a young-looking face through surgery while underneath your body is declining. Radical ways of rejuvenation must begin at the level of the cell. With RR you look great *before* you've put on your make-up – in fact you don't even need the stuff; you move like a young colt with or without a daily workout, your hair is shiny *before* you've put on the conditioner.

Do you want to know more?

And will you have to make drastic, even radical changes to your lifestyle? You bet. Is it worth it? Ditto. Even as you grit your teeth and call me names, you'll be smiling in the mirror. You'll probably be doing more smiling than you've done for a long time because this programme works. But there is a programme for cheats so don't despair.

HOW TO MAKE YOUR CELLS GROW YOUNGER

I don't know if I'm being poetic or scientific here – I always thought the best of science had a good deal of poetry in it. Whichever it turns out to be, science or poetry, there is a way to make your skin look younger, your body firmer and sexier and more supple, a way to turn flabby arms into sexy limbs and have you feeling the way you used to feel a long time ago. You'll notice sex creeping into most of what I say. This is because I like sex and also because I think vibrant sexuality is the direct result of effective rejuvenation. This 'way' is, of course, Radical Rejuvenation and it consists of the Radical Rejuvenation Diet, the Radical Rejuvenation Tonics and the Radical Rejuvenation Supplements. They all work but they *really* work together. I admit it's for desperados – but then aren't we all first thing in the morning, before the programme, that is.

THE RADICAL REJUVENATION DIET

This is the exact opposite of what you are eating now. I know this because if you were already eating this diet you wouldn't have to worry about wrinkles and other nasties. This diet will produce the opposite of what you've got – instead of wrinkles you'll get smooth, firm skin, instead of Visible Middle Age you'll get a head-turning body, instead of Early Nights you'll get lots of fun, especially if you put your man on the programme, too. And you won't wake up bleary eyed ever again.

The RR Diet is very simple. You just eat all your food raw and no animal foods of any sort (not even raw), no smoking, coffee, tea or alcohol. But that bit is obvious. It's the raw and the no animal bits that need explanation.

Animal products of any kind are responsible for all sorts of degenerative changes in the human body – those loose folds that sag around your mouth, flabby arms and a stomach that needs all those sit-ups to make it look good; infections, flu and colds – they are all indicative of a serious lack of vitality at the cellular level and they mean A-G-E-I-N-G. In fact, *all* cooked foods produce degenerative changes to some extent. Steamed vegetables are not as bad as a steak in cream sauce, but they are light years away from an all-raw way of eating all the same. No matter what you do to try and avoid it – eating raw foods before cooked, or eating half of your food cooked and half raw, or any other combination – the fact remains that any cooked foods in your diet will produce changes which will result in the changes we call ageing. The only diet which truly vitalises and renews your body is one which excludes all cooked and all animal foods. Try it. All you need is a little imagination and a whole world of tastes will open up to you.

Most people begin to see improvements from day two (i.e. after the first twenty-four hours on the RR Diet). But the full effects become obvious after four to six months, which means that if you're reading this in the winter then by the next hot summer you'll be enjoying seeing your reflection. If you are reading this in the summer, then at the time when everyone else will be pale, podgy and definitely uninteresting, you'll be glowing and definitely in a class of your own.

Radical Rejuvenation is fun – at least, I think that feeling and looking young and sexy is fun. Any programme which is fun has to have a chocolate substitute. I am speaking as one who once consumed chocolate for breakfast at 6 a.m.! A chocolate substitute has to be sweet and delicious and delightful, give you a wonderful lift and make you feel that life is definitely worth living. Well, this one does all that and it's non-fattening, too! It's carrot juice. Fresh and raw and delicious. Have it every day. Lots of times. You won't even miss all those spots you get from chocs.

THE RADICAL REJUVENATION TONICS

If you asked most people about the subjects most likely to raise a yawn, the workings of the internal organs must rate way up there with inspecting your ex-boyfriend's toenails. But if I told you that you look old because your liver is cracking up under its workload, you'd begin to find it a little more interesting. A good liver will give you a flatter stomach, firm skin around your eyes, good skin colour, balanced hormones, clear eyes. And there are herbs which will give you a good liver and good kidneys, adrenals, thymus and lungs. All very important for real, radical rejuvenation. These herbs are included in the programme and they work with and greatly enhance the good effects of the RR Diet.

THE RADICAL REJUVENATION SUPPLEMENTS OR HOW TO LOOK GOOD IN ANYTHING

There is a difference between looking young and looking thin. Everyone knows that kids can look good in anything – even a brown paper bag. That's the Youth Factor. If you've got it, it flaunts itself. Past thirty-five it's usually extinct.

Even if you're thin, you usually end up looking drawn rather than firm and juicy. Firm and juicy is what you get with RR. Especially when you add the RR Supplements to the RR Diet and Tonics. Because certain nutritional supplements have the ability to tone up your body from inside out, make you great in bed (my favourite area of rejuvenation), give you firm skin and muscles, thick hair, repair sun damage and generally make you look really good.

CHAPTER ONE

Skin Rejuvenation

I no longer worry about wrinkles. I have learnt to change the emphasis from wrinkles to skin rejuvenation. When you do that you find that wrinkles diminish in both importance and visibility. There is a myth which persists even though it is completely false and certainly doesn't do anyone any favours. This is a Big Depressing Myth which states that 'nothing at all can be done about wrinkles apart from cosmetic surgery'. Yet everywhere we look there is evidence of the amazing regenerating power of the human body – recoveries are made from 'terminal' cancer, cirrhosis of the liver has been shown to be reversible with milk thistle extracts, Alzheimer's has been slowed down with Ginkgo Biloba (now outselling aspirin in Germany). On a more basic level we have all seen the rapid beneficial changes that exercise can bring to flabby bodies, and hair responds dramatically to a good diet and mineral supplements as well as showing rapid and reversible deterioration during illness. Nothing to be done about wrinkles apart from the knife? Come on!

So what happens when you stop thinking wrinkles and start thinking face rejuvenation? You realise that you have much more control over the destiny of your face than you had previously thought. Skin Rejuvenation means that you approach your beauty care with a feeling of power, optimism and excitement. Pretty much all common problems can be improved or eradicated if you take charge and begin working with your body.

Skin Rejuvenation means also that you start with the basics. You work from inside out. This means that your face must be in great shape *before* you apply any make-up or skin treatments – oxygen, cell renewal and cell vitality are what we're talking about.

THE STRUCTURE OF YOUR FACE

Everyone knows what bad muscle tone looks like – most people over thirty-five have seen it close up. Flabby arms, loose flesh around the buttocks, a wrinkled midriff. If lack of tone can wrinkle your stomach, can it wrinkle your face, too? You bet it can! So this is the first thing to realise and it's positive too. The sags and bags that depress you when you look into the mirror are due to POOR MUSCLE TONE, i.e. a correctable reversible condition, and the reversal is accomplished by:

1. The RR Diet;
2. Supplements, especially full spectrum amino acids, herbs and enzymes;
3. A proper, good workout. Aerobics for the face no less.

FACIAL AEROBICS

Forget half-hearted stretching while you brush your teeth at bedtime, this is serious. It's also fun, mostly because it REALLY WORKS, so give it your best shot – bring all your energy and exhilaration to the task and you could be looking forward to meeting your reflection in a matter of days! This is why, in Skin Rejuvenation, we count reps in tens and hundreds, just like other fitness freaks. However, always take care to move the muscles precisely and accurately and avoid wrinkling and screwing up the rest of your face – you are strengthening your facial structure and there is nothing mindless or chaotic about it.

The Warm-up

This exercise is marvellous for toning up the large cheek muscles which are so prone to sagging Performed correctly, that is FAST but accurately, all the way and with no half-hearted movements, it does for your face in one or two minutes what rebounding on a trampoline does for the rest of you – it oxygenates your facial tissues very effectively. You know by now that oxygen is good for you. It is very good for you especially when it gets to your cells. This exercise gets it there.

Place your hands on either side of your face and then smile, revealing your teeth. Push your smile up as far as it can go, all the time resisting with your hands and preventing the rest of your face from creasing up. Perform one hundred times per session, FAST. Work up to five sessions if possible. (And it is!) As you get more advanced, you will feel a lightness come into your muscles during this exercise – it is the leanness that long-distance runners get in their legs and it's no less exhilarating just because it's in your face. It is the feeling of well-toned muscles and spells *aliveness*. One more thing – a bonus – facial muscles are very responsive and sensitive to training. It takes many hard hours of pavement pounding to get those long-distance legs but you can see and feel a difference in your face after just a few *days* of dedicated face aerobics. And you can do them anywhere: in the bath, on the loo, in bed. I hope you've run out of excuses now.

The Eyeliners

Why don't children have droopy eyelids? Because they have nice, firm muscles there instead, that's why. By the way, if you have bloodshot eyes and puffy eyelids and bags, too, you're looking at your liver and kidneys and it's all reversible. Liver tonics (barberry, milk thistle, He Shou Wu, burdock, yellow dock and Bupleurum) kidney tonics (especially Gou Qi Zi) and the RR Diet will work miracles around your eyes. These exercises are a little more superficial, but still well worth getting excited about. The first thing you'll realise when you first attempt these exercises is that I was right – poor muscle tone is what you've got if droops are your problem. But now you know it's no longer a problem, just a reason to get on with it. By the way, if all this talk of exercise is making you want to rush straight into the arms of the nearest cosmetic surgeon, you ought to know that even they are recommending face exercise after surgery to make their work last longer. If you become a face aerobics freak now (and follow the RR programme) you might never again yearn for surgery anyway! And while we're on the subject of eyes – a simple nightly application of castor oil to clean lashes repairs the damage caused by mascara. Some people (including myself) even swear that this treatment makes the eyelashes grow thicker and longer! So, for the exercise.

Place your two index fingers just underneath your brow bones and hold them there firmly. Support your elbows on a table top if possible. Now, without wrinkling your forehead, pull down the muscles of your upper eyelid until you have shut your eye, making those muscles work against the resistance of your fingers. At first you'll probably wonder where those muscles have got to – there won't be much muscle power there, but you'll soon build up a lot of strength and you'll feel just like all those famous people with biceps every time you flex your lids! Start fairly slowly on this one – this muscle tends to be pretty weak in most people, a little like stomach muscles on out-of-condition bodies. But starting slowly still means WORK – just do twenty instead of fifty repetitions. Your aim is fifty, or one hundred if you're aiming for trampoline-tight.

For the Under-eye Area

Place your index finger along the lower eye muscle and lift it strongly, against the resistance from your fingers. Repeat lots of times, preferably working up to fifty times each day.

For the Forehead Area

If you have frown lines and horizontal lines on your forehead, the first thing to do is to stop creating them, so no frowning or habitual eyebrow raising. Keep your forehead clear and serene like that of a beautiful Eastern princess. Or something. Secondly, moisturise this area well (see later in this chapter) and treat it gently; the skin here is particularly prone to drying out. Thirdly, perform regular and intensive pressure massage which will diminish the lines considerably and improve circulation and lymphatic drainage too. But, most importantly, as for all wrinkles and sags and bags anywhere on the body, which includes the face, get on to the full RR programme, using the RR Diet and Tonics and Supplements. As you will soon see, these three factors, even without face exercise and external treatments, will strengthen and firm facial and body tissue, improve circulation and oxygenation and the health of your cells (and this means face, too, of course), resulting in a face which you're happy to meet in the mirror (even first thing in the morning) and which looks good even without make-up – as it should.

To perform lymphatic drainage on your forehead, first place the heel of your hand between the eyebrows and press deeply. Hold for a moment and repeat. Perform twenty times. To smooth horizontal lines from the forehead, place the index, middle and ring fingers of your hands vertically across your forehead, fingertips facing, in the centre of the forehead (index finger is closest to the hairline). Apply firm pressure with all your fingers, then move them all outwards towards the temples, pressing in short bursts and working the whole area right up to the temples. Then repeat the sequence. Aim for twenty.

To Firm the Mouth

Form the letter 'O' with your lips and then press the muscles outwards. Repeat. Aim for fifty. Your mouth should ache after this!

The Pout

I am a great student of the pout. Especially since my own mouth almost disappeared under a deluge of lines and simply would *not* pout. I noticed *everybody's* mouth! And I learnt that little children have a lovely natural pout and that mouths get thinner with age. Children have wonderful muscle tone around the mouth; you can almost see the elastic, bouncy bands of muscle supporting their lips and making them stick out! So I decided to try some serious body building on my own, shrinking lips. The good news is that you *can* build up your pout! Maybe not all the way to notorious level, but you'll be pleased all the same. Like any exercise that's worthy of its name, this hurts! But not very much and not for long. The results, on the other hand, are wonderfully obvious and do last, though I would recommend regular workouts; as with all muscle training, the benefits will eventually disappear if you discontinue the training. Just remember that it *should* feel like 'work'.

Here is what you do. Sit at a table or on the bed so that you can support your elbows on the tabletop or your knees. Lean on your support and hook your index fingers under your lower lip, tips of fingers pointing down towards the floor. We're exercising the lower lip first. Push out slightly with your index fingers and hold. This provides the muscles of this area with sufficient resistance to work against, so remember not to relax the pressure. Now bring in the muscles of your lower lip towards your teeth *while pushing out* with your fingers. Each 'pull-in' of your lower lip counts as one repetition. Begin with twenty repetitions and quickly build up to one hundred. If you're really keen and want to see fast improvements, try to go for four hundred daily repetitions. It sounds a lot, but the movements are quite fast, so it doesn't take long once you have strengthened those lips! In the beginning you will need rests just like a runner who is out of breath. Because although the movements are small, they should be STRONG. Your mouth should ache! But the aching passes fast and you're left with a glow that doesn't fade, *if* you keep it up.

Now for the upper lip. It's the same principle as for the lower lip. Support your arms and hook your thumbs under your upper lip, push out with your fingers and pull in with your lip against this resistance. Your thumbs should be pointing up towards your eyes, nails facing your teeth, the soft pads touching the inside of your lip. Build up as for the lower lip. ALL mouths over thirty will love 'The Pout'!

To Firm a Jawline
(or to Keep a Firm One Looking Young)

Bend your head back as far as it will go, then open and close your mouth strongly. Make sure you feel a strong pull in your throat muscles. Aim for fifty repetitions.

Although Face Aerobics are very good, once you've been on the RR programme for six months or so, you will find that they are pretty much unnecessary. This is because the programme (the RR Diet, RR Tonics and RR Supplements) works to rejuvenate your cells. So, here is the Supersonic part of the Skin Rejuvenation Programme!

The Skin Rejuvenation Toolkit

The Radical Rejuvenation Diet
Essential Fatty Acids
Essential Oils
Radical Rejuvenation Tonics
Radical Rejuvenation Supplements

I hope you want sexy, glowing, moist, young skin which is soft all over (even on the knees and upper arms) and doesn't end at the neck! Because it's possible. This is how you do it:

THE RR DIET FOR SKIN REJUVENATION

Definitely. Nothing but raw foods if you want to look really fantastic and wrinkle-free, firm and young and, once you get over the shock of it, because it is so different to the food we're all used to, I'm sure you will come to love this new way of eating. Not least because of its effects!

A few general rules first:

- Eat all your nuts and seeds pre-soaked. This means a minimum of a couple of hours in pure water – it makes a lot of difference to how they feel in your body. Often nuts produce a feeling of heaviness and are very difficult to digest; not at all the sort of thing for youth and vitality. Pre-soaked they feel much lighter and more energising. Also the protein is made more available to your body. Experiment with all the nuts and seeds you can find (no roasted ones, though). Brazils are rich in calcium and the amino acid methionine (often scarce in vegan diets); pecans are madly delicious and contain useful quantities of vitamin C; sesame seeds contain lots of calcium as do almonds, which are also a good lung tonic; pumpkin seeds are rich in zinc, the skin mineral; hazelnuts and walnuts contain Omega 3 fatty acids which give you super soft skin and super shiny hair; sunflower seeds contain selenium which protects skin against damage from pollution and makes you feel good to boot.

- And don't worry about calories. Some people love calories. They love all those numbers going in and out, all those elaborate calculations. For good measure they also calculate Fat Exchange Units and Carbohydrate Exchange Units and probably also the surface area of the Moon, with and without the bumpy bits. I've seen lots of such people. When they go on diets they lose weight. Full stop. They look exactly the same as they did before the weight loss, except there's less of them. For goodness sake, you don't want to look the same, you want to look BETTER! And you don't want to look merely thin when you can look young. Calorie counting and the subsequent weight loss leave your Youth Index exactly where it was – your muscles don't look firm and rounded, the movement of your limbs is not more smooth and supple, often you have more wrinkles than you had when you started. You need a charge, not a game with calories. The RR Diet and the rest of the programme gives you that charge.

- Replace conventional sweeteners with dried fruit and honey. Even dried fruit in its concentrated form is sweet – teeth really do suffer from all forms of excessive sweetness and there is evidence that, further down the line, bones do, too. However you will soon find that fresh fruit really is sweet enough, especially if you explore the delights of tropical fruit. Dried fruit can be used (try to obtain organic dried fruit if you can; non-organic is often coated with mineral oil to make it shiny and less sticky – a definite no-no for great looks) and is delicious in fruity mixes; it's not as sweet when it is diluted in water. The best oils for salad dressings are cold-pressed walnut oil or hazelnut oil. Both contain Omega 3 essential fatty acids (walnuts are, in addition, also a good source of magnesium, which is wonderful for strong bones and nerves). Try this delicious blend any time you're hungry – it makes a great breakfast: blend organic sultanas with some fresh fruit such as bananas, add a whole lemon, cut into slices, with peel (some of the residual pesticides can be removed if you soak fruit and veg in some water to which you've added organic cider vinegar, then rinse well afterwards), one small peeled beetroot (I know I sound like a maniac – raw beetroot! But it's delicious, trust me) and one or two carrots. Blend well, in stages as written here, i.e. first the water and sultanas, then the lemon and so on. You can also add pre-soaked nuts or seeds of your choice mixed in with the dried fruit in the first step and if you have Gou Qi Zi berries (more about these in the chapter on herbs) add those, too. You could easily live on this for the rest of your life and look fantastic.

Strictly speaking, dried fruit is not, actually, raw, because organic fruits are deep frozen to kill off bugs and sun-dried non-organic fruit is washed and then dried again, this time in ovens. This is the one exception to the iron all-raw rule. You can use dried fruit sparingly on the RR Diet, especially when you are starting out. However, that old raw-food staple, carob flour, doesn't appear in the RR Diet because it is roasted – sometimes only lightly, but roasted nevertheless. Oats are another food which is heat processed when you might expect it to be raw – even oatmeal has been steamed, as have porridge oats and, often, the whole groats, too. This makes for an enzyme-deficient product which will not produce radiance. You will find more information on raw foods in Chapter Ten. These foods are fine if you are not going for the Gold Band (see page 227), or during the transition from cooked foods to raw foods, but they will not produce Radical Rejuvenation so you need to be aware from the start that 'raw' quite often isn't! Even olives are pasteurised. Thank God our fresh produce has escaped irradiation, is all I can say! And don't worry, there are still plenty of delicious things left to eat, as you will see in Chapter Eleven.

- If you use herbs and spices (and you should), make sure they have not been heat processed – some of the famous super-market ones have been subjected to high temperatures. Use dulse flakes instead of salt. Again, make sure the dulse is just dried, not heat processed in any way – most dulse is, to my knowledge, simply dried, but some products containing it may have been heated.

You will find a more detailed description of the RR Diet in Part Three which includes hints and ideas for recipes, too.

ESSENTIAL FATTY ACIDS (EFAs)

I'm an oil freak. EFAs, UFAs, GLA, Omega 3, Omega 6 – I love them all. (I don't use fish oils because I don't eat animal products. Animal products just don't produce stunning looks.) If you try them you will soon see why I say that anyone seriously interested in looking young and gorgeous has to include them in their daily programme. Don't worry about your waistline – these oils have very different effects from the fats we're all used to, the saturated kind found in butter, cheese, milk and meat. In fact, used correctly, these magical oils of vegetable origin can trim your stomach and even make your breasts bigger while leaving the rest of you nice and firm and slender. Interested? Then here's my top six.

The Top Six Oils for Skin Rejuvenation

Most people think of moisturisers and hair conditioners as an everyday necessity and they are – because most people are deficient in essential fatty acids, or EFAs. EFAs are as essential for your health as vitamins and minerals, and more essential for good looks than any cosmetic anyone is ever likely to produce. After just two weeks of consistent daily use (and often much sooner) you'll notice it – incredibly soft, elastic skin ALL over and hair which is shiny and lovely and stays clean for longer between washes. Here are the six most important sources of these important beautifiers:

WALNUT OIL

This one's number one. Just two large spoonfuls a day are all you need for great skin and you can use more if you can afford it! It tastes great and there's nothing to beat it in a salad dressing. Just make sure it's unrefined and cold-pressed, always store it in the fridge and as soon as you open the bottle add 3000 i.u. (international units) of vitamin E to prevent oxidation and to supply your body with this important vitamin every time you take your walnut oil. Add 20 drops of BioCare's VitaSorb C for the same reason. When taking EFAs you must have an adequate intake of vitamin E and adding it directly to the bottle ensures that your minimum needs are met. Shake the bottle well before each use. You will find a list of recommended products and suppliers at the end of this book. By the way, it's a good idea to add vitamin E and vitamin C to all your bottles of oil, whichever you choose.

Walnut oil is a good source of Omega 3 EFAs, which are quite scarce in the normal Western diet. You can also use it externally – just mix it with some good essential oils (see following section) and you've got a far better rejuvenating treatment than the most expensive creams on the market! Mixed with some zinc oxide powder (you can buy that from the chemist) it makes a simple and effective (if a little on the white side – experiment with concentrations) sunscreen. Your skin will feel smooth and silky after every use and since both zinc and walnut oil are so beneficial for your skin you can use it every day. As you should – studies have shown that, if a sunscreen is worn every day, not only will you prevent sun damage, your skin will actually repair existing damage, too. If you add some vitamin E to this sunscreen (so that you have about 200 i.u. per application) and take the vitamin internally (about 200 i.u.) you will further increase the skin-regenerating effects of this treatment. For more supplements which enhance skin regeneration, see the section on RR Supplements later in this chapter. By the way, don't take excessive amounts (in the range of 400 i.u. daily and above) without consultation with a knowledgeable nutritionist. Vitamin E can increase blood pressure in some people.

Taken internally, this lovely oil will condition your skin and hair. If you have stiff joints, just one or two large spoonfuls can work wonders, as long as you help your body by cutting down on animal products, especially dairy foods. Externally this oil makes a great conditioner for the skin and hair. Use the oil before you shampoo your hair and wash it several times with a good shampoo such as the ones recommended in the chapter on lifestyle. Rinse well with clear water and your hair will look and feel wonderful. Walnut oil also makes a great pre-shampoo conditioner. Use two or three good washes and rinse well. Your hair will be wonderful!

HAZELNUT OIL

Wickedly yummy and terribly expensive, use it when you have special friends coming round or for pure self-indulgence when you're feeling low. It transports any salad into the Concorde Class effortlessly. It's also rich in Omega 3 EFAs which means that this treat is GOOD for you! Use it as you would walnut oil on face and hair – it smells so delicious your man just might decide to eat *you* instead of the salad.

LINSEED OIL

A much more serious affair this one. This one *tastes* like it's good for you and it is. A very good source of Omega 3 and Omega 6 fatty acids. Make sure it's cold-pressed and very fresh; if it tastes bitter it's off – throw it out. You will find some of the best suppliers in the section at the back of the book. This oil may also be used externally with superb results, but since it doesn't smell as divine as hazelnut oil or as nice as walnut oil, you might not be as tempted to cover yourself in it. Try it anyway. It's an oil worth being nice to! And this is *the* best rejuvenating oil I've ever tried on my face. Linseed oil is also known as flax seed oil.

EVENING PRIMROSE OIL

This one's famous. It's so good for you it's a wonder it's not illegal. Actually, it is available on prescription, which just goes to show. This is the oil that can make your boobs bigger while leaving the rest of you as slender as you love to be, makes you an angel before your periods, softens your skin and hair and generally is a Good Thing. It contains gamma linolenic acid or GLA, an Omega 6 essential fatty acid also found in borage oil. My favourite way to take it is to dispense with all those gelatine capsules and buy it, very fresh, in pure liquid form. It tastes mild and slightly sweet – quite delicious, in fact. Sometimes I pour about 50 ml into my bottle of walnut and vitamin E mix and use it straight from the fridge to speed up the process of taking supplements (which can be lengthy).

BORAGE OIL

Borage oil contains a higher concentration of GLA than evening primrose oil, and has caused quite a bit of excitement in the beauty industry because it has been found to stimulate cell oxygenation. It's a pleasant and mild oil with effects very similar to evening primrose and makes a lovely base for a skin-firming treatment. It's very light and easily absorbed; just a few drops rubbed on to your hair before you wash it will condition and feed it wonderfully. If you buy it pure, in larger quantities than you get in capsules, you can rub it all over and feel its rejuvenating effects on your whole body. It feels refreshing and energising.

AVOCADO OIL

If you can find cold-pressed, unrefined avocado oil, then use that, otherwise indulge in lots of avocados daily and use them mashed as a face, neck and hand treatment, as well as a pre-shampoo hair treatment. Avocados have been found to contain a factor which stimulates the production of fresh skin cells. Avocado oil is a green, viscous, beautiful oil which is fantastic on your skin and hair. For best effects eat the avocados whole and use either the oil or the mashed pulp externally.

ESSENTIAL OILS

It must be pretty obvious by now that plants, used both externally and internally, contain very potent rejuvenating substances. For the purposes of skin rejuvenation, the essential oils made from aromatic plants are remarkable. They can firm up saggy skin, enhance cell renewal and diminish wrinkles. I adore them – they're almost as good as being in love. I have a whole cupboardful, or so it seems, because every time I open it I am greeted by their delectable smell. My favourite ones just happen to be real rejuvenation dynamos. An important rule to remember is that you should always dilute essential oils in a carrier oil such as walnut or avocado before applying to your skin. If you are pregnant, check with a health professional before using any essential oils, herbs or other supplements. And don't take essential oils internally – they may sound similar to essential fatty acids, but they are not. For our purposes the external application of essential oils is more than adequate to perform magic! Also, keep all essential oils away from the eye area. As far as makes are concerned, I think Tisserand is the Rolls-Royce of essential oils. Tisserand oils are widely available in health food shops.

The Top Eight Essential Oils for Skin Rejuvenation

ROSE

No matter what, this one has to be first. It's exquisite, feminine, delectable, powerfully rejuvenating and horribly expensive. It rebalances hormones, makes you feel beautiful, gets you smiling and smoothes your skin noticeably after just one week of faithful use. It's a pleasure to use. If you can only buy one essential oil, save up for rose. It comes as an absolute or as Otto. The latter has slightly stronger effects but I prefer the scent of the absolute. Use it by itself as a perfume or treatment, and diluted in one of the oils from the above section (for example walnut) as a skin regenerator.

BENZOIN

If it weren't for rose, this would be my favourite oil. The balsamic and woody oils (benzoin, myrrh, frankincense, sandalwood, rosewood and cedarwood) have wonderful effects: rejuvenating on the skin and mellow and harmonising on the emotions (although rosewood is commonly used as an emotional stabiliser and cedarwood is mostly used in hair care, they are all nevertheless rejuvenators). Benzoin is excellent at tightening loose skin. It smells divine, very reminiscent of vanilla, and has other qualities important for rejuvenation which you will find mentioned in the chapter on sex! Rough and irritated skin responds marvellously to benzoin; try it on dermatitis and excema. As well as firming your body and face, benzoin is great at regenerating sun-damaged skin and dissolving small cysts (you may apply the oil undiluted to the cyst).

MYRRH

One of the most respected rejuvenators for women in the ancient Indian healing science of Ayurveda, myrrh has a long and distinguished history as a youth maker. If you combine it with the rest of the RR programme, you will find that its reputation is well deserved. The programme allows all these oils and herbs and supplements to work at the very highest and most effective level. Often very effective products are taken by people whose lifestyle and diet work against their positive effects. Myrrh has very strong firming qualities; it is excellent for saggy breasts or cheeks that need tightening up. It is also superb at smoothing out wrinkles. I love the smell of myrrh and I love its effects; I have taken it in tincture form internally and externally and have used the essential oil frequently and can report very good results. For more on myrrh, see the chapter entitled 'How to Have a Sexy Body'.

FRANKINCENSE
In the same family as myrrh and benzoin, this is another balsamic firming rejuvenator. It has a warming, smoky scent which makes it an intriguing and attractive addition to your face oil. By the time you've finished, you will have a beautiful perfume as well as a skin treatment!

LEMON
After all those smouldering, sexy, balsamic numbers, we come to jolly old citrusy lemon. But don't let that fool you – friendly and familiar it may be, but lemon knows what it's doing; whether in the form of lemon juice (fresh) or when added to your skin treatment oils, lemon will: bleach brown pigmentation, smooth wrinkles, increase production of fresh, new cells and generally brighten your skin. It's great on blonde hair, too. Be careful, though, and never use it before going out into the sun. (This applies to all citrus oils, including bergamot. Never use sun products containing these oils. They do speed up tanning, but the cost can be great – unsightly brown blotches which are very difficult to remove.)

JASMINE
You can't talk about rejuvenating essential oils and leave this one out. When it's really really pure its scent alone makes you feel like a young girl. It starts things from inside out; definitely radical. It balances hormones and calms you and your skin and leaves you smiling and glowing. Smiling's very rejuvenating I think.

YLANG YLANG
Similar to jasmine and rose (but less expensive), ylang ylang is another

flower oil with a special ability to make women look and feel beautiful. Like most of the oils mentioned so far, it is also an aphrodisiac. I like aphrodisiacs. They are fantastic rejuvenators, not least because they balance hormonal secretions and improve the vitality and efficiency of all your systems, down to the smallest cell. Ylang ylang balances and harmonises oil production in the skin, so if your skin is too dry (and it is after thirty-five, at least in places) it will become moist, not simply because you have added an external lubricant but because your own lubricating system has been boosted. And if you have areas which are too oily, ylang ylang will normalise them, too. Which is how it should be, with true tonics and rejuvenators.

LAVENDER

One of the most powerful and reliable cell regenerating oils, lavender stimulates your skin and gets it moving in the right direction – heading towards smooth and wrinkle-free and fresh and young. It's mild enough to use neat and yet effective enough to make a safe first-aid burn treatment.

THE RADICAL REJUVENATION TONICS

Most people are aware that a good diet is an essential for great looks; the RR Diet, though unusual, makes sense as an effective means of rejuvenation. But many people are simply not aware of the magic hidden in certain plants. Many Western people I should say, because the plants which are used in the RR programme have been revered in the East for centuries precisely because of the powerful effects that they produce on the human body. We're not talking camomile tea bags here; the plants used for rejuvenation are in a class of their own. Used regularly as part of the RR programme, they will contribute strongly towards a more youthful, fresh complexion. You will find more details on the use and properties of herbs, including precautions, in Chapter Nine. Here are some of the best herbs for skin rejuvenation:

Top Tonics

HE SHOU WU

Removes wrinkles, restores grey hair to its original colour, regrows teeth, increases life span. Interesting herb. I hold this one very dear to my heart and believe it is capable of all of the above *if* the root is good enough. Which means very dark and strong and old and rare. Don't smirk – even with the Western quality roots I have seen colour restored to grey hair and a remarkable improvement in the quality of aged skin. After only three months, too. I adore everything about this herb, from the taste of the powder, to the look of the cut root and the taste of the tincture. Get to know it. It deserves to be at least as popular as ginseng – and it isn't expensive. By the way, look for it by its Latin name, *Polygonum multiflorum*. It's less confusing when trying to figure out whether Fo Ti is the same as He Shou Wu and Fo Ti Tieng and where Gotu Kola comes in. (If you really want to know, some people call He Shou Wu by the name of Fo Ti and some people call Gotu Kola, a completely different plant, *Centella asiatica* in Latin and not related to Kola, by the name Fo Ti Tieng. So now you know. This is why God made herbalists, they like working out this sort of thing.) If you can, try every single sort of He Shou Wu and decide which one you like best, and if you can't decide, use them all! For more on the mysterious He Shou Wu see the chapter entitled 'How to Be Great in Bed'. As I said, I like this plant.

SCHIZANDRA

It's pink, tastes like Cinzano, improves cell oxygenation, makes your skin rosy and smooth and even turns you on. The tincture of Schizandra, that is. You can buy it in powder form but I find the alcoholic preparation so much more fun! (By the way, when using tinctures which do contain alcohol, we are talking about very small amounts – it certainly would be detrimental to drink tinctures, however medicinal, in quantities bigger than the recommended teaspoon doses.) The advantage of taking herbs in tincture form is that the effects are faster and stronger and it's often a more convenient way of taking them than powder or tea. However, a tincture is not quite the same as the whole herb and this may be a disadvantage – if the active principle(s) is not soluble in alcohol, for example. With Wu Wei Zi (the Chinese name for Schizandra) this is not a problem – the tincture is gloriously effective. As with all herbs, take it for at least three months, though the results should be felt long before that time is up. (Many people have taken Schizandra and herbs such as the ones described in this book throughout their life with very good results. You can think of herbs as a sort of Superfood.) Some people find the effects of herbs subtle; they just know that, somehow, they feel and look better and often don't give credit where credit is definitely due – to the herbs. Others, myself included, feel the power of these herbs a bit like vitality dynamos. It doesn't really matter – as long as you're feeling better and looking great, who cares if it creeps up on you or hits you over the head?

DANG GUI

All beautiful women ought to take Dang Gui (and that's all of us, right?). It is variously known as Tang Kwei, Dang Gui and, in Latin, *Angelica sinensis* or *chinensis.* It is an Eastern relative of our very own green, sugared angelica, and what a difference a few thousand miles can make! Dang Gui is POWERFUL and softens you all over – inside and out, emotions and looks, and while softening it strengthens, which is not really a paradox at all (told you it was the herb for women). I usually feel its effects from dose one and so should you – if you are clear enough and if you've got a high quality product. And the test of a good product? If you don't feel *sexy* after the first mouthful, then it isn't it. Give it a go for a few more days and, if nothing happens, find another make. I love taking Dang Gui in tincture and cut root form; it has an unusual but a nice taste. Take a teaspoon of the tincture or a slice of the root twice a day. Get ready to shine!

CHLORELLA AND SPIRULINA

The first thing you'll notice when you begin taking either or both of these rejuvenators is that you really look *good*; you know the thing – shiny hair, really shiny, soft moist skin, shiny eyes. And your energy is just fantastic and you keep grinning at people for no reason. Both chlorella and spirulina are full of all sorts of goodies, such as RNA/DNA, chlorophyll, vitamins and minerals. All good anti-ageing stuff and they work fast. I've seen people (though admittedly in very good health) look better overnight after taking chlorella. Most people will have to wait longer for results. But not very long and results are what you get. Take enough (one teaspoon three times a day at least) and go for quality; Chlorella Health, for instance, is very good. They recommend twelve tablets as the daily dose and I find that to be sufficient. However, as both chlorella and spirulina are foods rather than concentrated supplements, I prefer going over the top and using lots. I feel good that way!

Liver and Kidney Tonics

Puffy, bloodshot eyes? Bags? Loose flesh? You're looking at your liver and kidneys. And you need dandelion, barberry, turmeric, burdock, yellow dock, He Shou Wu, Bupleurum, milk thistle and Gou Qi Zi. These herbs will tighten the area around your eyes, remove redness and make your eyes sparkle like crazy. You can throw away those chemical eye drops.

HOW TO USE THE LIVER HERBS

The fastest way to cleanse and stimulate the liver is to go on the RR Diet and drink the following tea, warm, three times a day. (Some herbal teas are much more effective taken hot and, for some reason, do not have the deleterious effects of cooked food. Other teas are best cold; some herbs work best raw and powdered, others as tinctures.)

Take one heaped teaspoon of barberry bark (not the same as bayberry nor bearberry!), cut or powdered, add one level teaspoon of turmeric powder and one of Bupleurum pieces (optional). Add three mugfuls of pure water, bring to the boil and simmer for twenty minutes. Strain and drink warm, divided into three doses each day for one week. Avoid barberry if you are pregnant or breast feeding.

After the first week, following the above liver cleanse, choose a good liver tonic. It could be dandelion root, but make sure it is dried, not roasted as well – it's more effective medicinally that way. Also add burdock root or yellow dock root; or a mixture of any or all of them. Make them into 'coffee' if you have cut pieces of root, or take them powdered in warm water, or a teaspoon of tincture. Again, take three doses a day. This step in the programme should take two weeks.

Step three consists of taking powdered milk thistle seed in a little bit of water every day (one dose is sufficient) as a liver regenerator and protector. Adding He Shou Wu powder will add more liver-strengthening compounds. Wild yam is a good tincture to add at this stage in the liver-strengthening programme, especially if irritability and PMT trouble you – this herb balances oestrogen and progesterone (but in favour of progesterone which is beneficial for nervous women who suffer from PMT) as well as being good for the liver.

Adding bitter herbs, such as dandelion greens, dried or fresh, gentian tincture or Swedish Bitters tincture, before every meal is also a good idea for toning the liver.

I know it sounds outrageous, but this programme of liver cleansing and regeneration, combined with the correct diet (the RR Diet, of course!) produces amazing changes in the face and body. I've seen flatter stomachs, firmer skin, bags and pouches and under-eye creases disappear, bloodshot eyes replaced by a youthful, clear sparkle.

And talking of sparkling, beautiful, youthful eyes, if you want some, you must take Gou Qi Zi (pronounced Goo-Chee-Zee and known by the Latin names *Lycium barbarum* or *Lycium chinensis*). These are small, sweet, red berries. They are delicious and make a great addition to your daily mix (see page 17). In less than four weeks you'll have the nicest eyes you've ever had!

THE RADICAL REJUVENATION SUPPLEMENTS

I suppose you think you've done enough now! But if you want to be the sexiest, youngest and best looking you for miles around (and at every party you go to!), read on. Here are more secrets for a face you're happy to wake up to – juicy, fresh and young.

The Number One Supplements

If you can only invest in one RR Supplement, make it this one. On top of all the other good things you'll be doing, this one produces magic. I have never seen such firm, youthful faces, great legs and strong bodies and muscles as when this was added to the programme. ('Added' is the operative word here – we're going for the *best*, which means using everything that works. Synergy is what happens when you use it all – and great looks are what you get.) It may seem expensive, especially when you only buy the best, which you must do for the right effects. Save up, steal or borrow, if you must. It's called BioScience Full Spectrum Aminos and you may have to get it through a practitioner or the Nutri Centre (address at the end of the book). It is worth more than every penny, so get some. A little bit of semi-scientific blurb here; you know by now that you need protein for muscles and hair and nails and skin because every magazine has been telling you that since you were in your teens. Amino acids are why you need protein – but what your hair usually gets is a complex mix of fat and animal protein which those magazines tell you are what you need. Meat, cheese, fish. That's not exactly how your body sees it – protein from animal sources isn't easy for your body to use; it has to be digested and broken down into its constituent amino and only then is it a useful product. The trouble is, most people's digestion, plus the fact that our bodies are happier dealing with proteins of vegetable origin, means that a lot of this protein is never used by the body for building and repair and creates, instead, unspeakable, ageing havoc inside, all too visible outside.

But when you supply these amino acids in their pure and therefore highly usable form, miracles begin to happen. You get that muscle definition that ten-year-olds have effortlessly because their bodies are at peak efficiency. Unless they are eating a 'normal, balanced diet' in which case they are already on their way to ruin. With Full Spectrum Free Form Aminos you get a firm, fresh face like the one you used to have back then, when you worried about being beautiful, not about looking young. When you didn't 'look your age'. And going backwards is what this is all about. Going backwards to look good and young rather than going forwards to wrinkles and flab, where everyone else is going.

And, *please*, don't be tempted to get protein powder, which is milk powder or dried egg powder with horrid things such as sugar, flavouring and synthetic vitamins in useless quantities. It will make you fat and old, not firm and young.

Of the proper stuff, take one teaspoon with each meal. More if you can afford it. Mix it with some spirulina or chlorella powder, raw veggies, a little Celtic sea salt, black pepper and water for a refreshing raw soup. In a week or two, you'll be walking into walls as you admire your reflection in shop windows. Not to mention gazing in unbelieving surprise into the mirror!

Vitamins and Minerals

Whole books have been written on this subject alone and very fine books they are. You can make this subject as complicated or as simple as you wish. So I'll make it simple. What matters is what you take and theory isn't going to make you young.

For wrinkle-free, smooth skin, protected from pollution and the sun, here is what you need:

With breakfast: One good multivitamin and multimineral formula which does not contain iron or copper but which includes B12. Take your iron supplement with supper. You usually don't need additional copper. BioCare make my favourite multivitamin and multimineral. Add BioCare's Mag 2:1 Cal, or one capsule of Magnesium EAP2 with one of Calcidophillus or Calcium EAP2, team it up with half a teaspoon of pure ascorbic acid powder from Boots, some lecithin granules from Solgar, make your mix and you're set. Don't forget the walnut oil. Straight from the spoon if you're made of stern stuff. I must admit that I throw *everything* into the blender like a peasant. With lots of bananas and sultanas you can (almost) not taste it. But then, I am a maniac and I make my whole family eat all this stuff! Still, I'm sure you'll find your own best way of getting all this in. By the way, and this is important, do note that at the present time (though it is changing) most vitamins and other supplements come in gelatine capsules. That means boiled horse's hooves! Not the sort of thing famed for its rejuvenative powers. So buy powders wherever possible – tip the contents out of the capsule and throw the capsule in the bin. It belongs there, not in your body. Also squeeze out the contents of a beta carotene capsule (BioCare) to give you 7500 i.u., and four drops of VitaSorb E (200 i.u. BioCare).

Supper: Take one iron EAP2 (BioCare) with a little bit of vitamin C (ascorbic acid powder from Boots). You don't need much vitamin C, just a little to enhance absorption of the iron and give you a lift.

Bedtime: If possible at least one hour after food, take one-half of a zinc citrate tablet (BioCare).

Here are the goodies your skin gets from this multi package:

- *B complex* (in the multi-capsule) delivers help for almost every single thing your skin could wish for from anti-wrinkling action to improving tone and balancing oil production, reducing the tendency to spots and blackheads and evening out skin tone by getting rid of those unsightly red blotches which form especially around greasy noses (sounds terrible, but it does happen, even on 'normal', balanced diets.)
- *Selenium* prevents and repairs damage caused by pollution and the sun, minimising wrinkles and making you feel happy into the bargain (also in the multivit).
- *Silica* (in the multivit) is a structuriser extraordinaire – with plenty of this stuff your face will never droop. It also does lovely things to your hair and nails.
- *Vitamin E* has been shown to repair skin wrinkled by the sun when used both internally and externally. More on externals in a minute.
- *Vitamin C* helps in the manufacture of collagen, which has been unpoetically termed 'skin glue' but it does hold the skin and all of you together and strengthen skin structure. Vitamin C also does great things when applied directly to the skin and a very special preparation is available. It's described in the following section.
- *Iron* improves oxygen utilisation.
- *Zinc*, well, zinc really knows what it's doing when it comes to skin

elasticity. It's so good at this elasticity game that if you take it during pregnancy (under qualified supervision) you will completely avoid getting those stretch marks. They result from poor elasticity – skin tearing because of lack of flexibility.

The programme given here is very effective in bringing about repair and youthfulness in your skin. Should you wish to further enhance its effects you can add the amino acid cysteine, in addition to the complete blend you are already taking which also strengthens and repairs wrinkled, sun-damaged skin. Take it first thing in the morning, about half an hour before breakfast, with some magnesium and a B complex (both from BioCare, half a capsule or a capsule of each). You can also increase the quantity of vitamin E to 400 i.u. gradually, by 50 i.u. each week, but don't take this quantity for more than three months. After this time, decrease it again to the maintenance dose of 200 i.u. by taking it down in 50 i.u. increments. Some vitamins and minerals can be toxic in high doses. Always consult a professional practitioner if you are pregnant, lactating or thinking about taking doses higher than those recommended here, which are well within the safety limits for adults. Vitamins are discussed more fully in Chapter Eight.

EXTERNAL REJUVENATION

I love plastering things on my face, body and hair. Especially things which are edible and things which work. I find that combination absolutely irresistible and the beauty of this RR approach is that if you have any leftovers from lunch you can mash them up for a quick, effective face pack or hair treat, and if you have any face pack or conditioner left you can turn it into a snack or lunch! Mad? You bet! Your neighbours will probably think you're funny but you'll look better than them, so who cares. So get ready for some really effective and horribly messy skin rejuvenators and some not so messy, just plain effective.

You don't need to worry about skin types, either. The best way of looking at ageing skin is in terms of regeneration and, strangely enough, when you use these rejuvenating treatments not only will you find an improvement in the tender, sensitive and wrinkled areas, you will also find that patches which were previously covered in blackheads look finer and better, using the same treatments.

Roxy's Favourite External Skin Rejuvenators

ENZYMES

We have to start with this one because it's as good as fruit acids and you don't have to take out a second mortgage to try it. I've tested lots of different, biologically active enzymes and the only one worth bothering with is Spectrumzyme, even though it contains lactase and your skin doesn't contain lac*tose* and so does not need this enzyme. But this doesn't matter at all because Spectrumzyme is fantastic when applied to the skin (it's not bad in other ways, too, by the way; see Chapter Three 'How to Have a Sexy Body'). Simply mix the contents of one Spectrumzyme capsule with a little water in the palm of your hand and apply to your face and neck and hands and anywhere else where you would like to have young, fresh looking skin. You might need more enzyme powder at this stage. Rinse well. Simple. Spectrumzyme is available from BioCare. Even though Spectrumzyme contains papain and bromelain, I have found it to be vastly superior to both papaya and pineapple, from which these enzymes are usually derived, as well as better than the commercial products containing the extracts from these fruits and there seems to be no reddening or peeling of the skin either, when you use Spectrumzyme. You just end up with clear, bright, smooth skin and smoothed out wrinkles. However, if your skin is sensitive use Spectrumzyme in low concentrations. Try a third or even less of the contents of one capsule mixed with a third of a cup of water and rinse after a few moments.

VITAMINS

Still on the civilised treatment, vitamins E and C make fantastic rejuvenators. You need to use a good vitamin E (such as VitaSorb E from BioCare) and a skin-active form of vitamin C. BioCare do two products which are suitable: VitaSorb C and Derma C cream. I prefer VitaSorb C for skin care. The C is a little yellow and sticky and E will feel warm and sticky but these minor irritations are well worth putting up with forever to get the results. Simply apply, gently, a few drops of each vitamin to all the wrinkled and wrinkle prone areas of your face, neck and hands, including under eyes, upper eyelids and frown lines. Don't leave out your hands; they age too and often need a little help. You can wipe off or rinse the excess after ten minutes or so, if you wish.

Most people notice a big improvement with this regime after three weeks. If you don't, carry on. It will come. Don't stop. If you don't want wrinkles, that is. By the way, I have noticed that VitaSorb C, when applied to the mouth and the lines above the lips, not only erases those lines very quickly, but also makes the lips much plumper and fuller.

ZINC

If your skin was always protected from the sun, it wouldn't wrinkle much at all. Even skin already damaged by the sun will begin to repair if it is protected by a sunscreen. The trouble is, most sunscreens contain a whole cacophony of chemicals which your skin doesn't need and doesn't want. So – here's how to make your own. It's effective and it's very white. But you can spread it around and try out different concentrations (nothing too technical – a bit less powder, a bit more oil, you know the sort of thing) until you achieve a shade that won't cause shrieks of laughter from your friends. Zinc oxide is the powder which will be doing the skin protection and walnut oil or sesame oil (cold-pressed, unrefined) are what you mix it with. And it's so much more than a sunscreen – your face will feel fantastic even after you have washed it. Because this sunscreen really conditions your skin and firms it, too. Apply it to all exposed areas and re-apply after a swim.

The whiter it is, the more protection you're getting. Just ignore your howling friends or dilute it a little and spread it more thinly around your face; it will still work.

HOTCH POTCH

Since we seem to have entered the territory of treatments which will result in mirth, laughter and ridicule, we may as well continue. They'll soon be asking you for your secrets, anyway.

Mashed avocado pulp is good. So are jojoba oil, sesame oil and avocado oil, even though they are not very messy. Add spirulina and you have a very shriek-worthy face pack and very effective. Lemon juice tightens the skin – apply it after you've oiled your skin. Salt can be used on oiled skin as an exfoliating treatment. Go gently; it is very effective.

PURE, FRESH, RAW PLANT JUICES

Probably the most neglected skin rejuvenators in the world. Processing and packaging renders them useless, which means that you can do better than the most fancy cosmetics houses and just for a few pence, too.

The best juice of all is obtained from horsetail – *Equisetum arvense* – packed with silica and capable of producing some of the most remarkable rejuvenating effects I've ever seen. Make sure of your plant though; some varieties of horsetail are poisonous. Just take the fresh plant and blend it with some water, then strain. You can drink a small amount, too, and it will supply you with much needed, firming silica; about one large spoonful is sufficient for one day.

Other good juices come from dandelion leaves, which can be blended with some water and strained; carrots, which are easiest juiced in a juicer; and nettles, which can be prepared as dandelion and horsetail above. Be careful when collecting the fresh nettles but the juice doesn't sting at all. Nettles are rich in silica and other minerals. Other juices to try are comfrey, watercress, parsley and spinach, even fresh orange and grape juice. Black grape juice is lovely. All of these are very beneficial internally, too. Use them regularly. You'll be astonished at their effectiveness in restoring tone and smoothness to your skin. Even tummies can be tightened and legs firmed!

ANOTHER GOODIE FOR YOU TO TRY –
ROSA MOSQUETA

I tried it and I like, I like! It's got a great pedigree: lots of EFAs; it comes from the fruit of a wild South American rose. Rosehips have been traditionally used in herbal medicine to stimulate skin health by increasing circulation and cell production. For this purpose they were ground into a fine powder and, mixed with a little water, gently rubbed over the face, then rinsed off. You can obtain rosehip shell powder from the Herbal Apothecary; the address is given at the back of the book. This oil has a similar effect but it's not drying, of course, so it's great for all of us who need to treat our skin with care.

Other oils you may wish to try are: jojoba, which, amazingly, doesn't leave a greasy film on your skin and also doesn't go rancid as it is a wax, not an oil; carrot seed oil which has a strong reputation as an anti-ager; and evening primrose oil. Try them all and use them on different days – your skin thrives on this sort of varied, adventurous diet. Just like the rest of you.

WHAT ABOUT THE PRODUCTS YOU ARE USING NOW?

The problem with normal, commercial soaps and shampoos is the lather, foam and bubbles. These products contain strong detergents which are very damaging to cells. In fact, there is some suggestion that these detergents, which are also found in washing-up liquids, even biodegradable ones, may be responsible, at least in part, for the great increase in food allergies which has recently occurred. The detergents damage the delicate mucosal lining of the gut, causing porosity and a leakage of undigested or partially digested material into the blood-stream, causing these allergic symptoms.

Try to protect your skin, body and hair from the effects of detergents as much as you can. There are safe alternatives for all detergent products. You will find them discussed in detail in Chapter Ten.

Fruit Acids

Even the hermits in the Himalayas probably have their own pots of the stuff nowadays. Fruit acids are big and they work. They are also very expensive. In their natural form they have been used by beauty witches for centuries. Yogurt, sour cream and sour milk, lemon juice, grape juice and red wine have been used for a long time to improve the complexion of beautiful women. It took twentieth-century methods to tell us that what these effective skin treatments have in common is something known as fruit acids or alpha hydroxy acids, AHAs for short. These acids take many forms. For instance, citric acid comes from lemons, tartaric acid from grapes and lactic acid from sour milk products. There is also glycolic acid.

Fruit acids have the power to make your skin look younger, smoother and firmer. At least a part of their action is due to the fact that they 'unstick' the glued-up surface skin cells which have got themselves into this messy state through loss or function. As cells age (and due to the detrimental changes wreaked by free radicals) they become clumped on the surface of the skin instead of being shed smoothly and easily to make room for fresh, new skin. This defective process leads to dry, scaly, unsightly patches. Most people call it 'dry' skin and apply 'moisturisers' and other oily substances to the skin in the hope of correcting the problem. But, as you can see, we are *not* talking about a situation which requires oil. In fact, this is a case of too *much* gluey, sticky stuff already! (You will find more about this in the following section.) This is why ordinary moisturisers based on oils and waxes, no matter how 'natural', often make no impact on aged, dry skin. What is needed is a bit of deconstruction to make way for subsequent healthy function. Enter the fruit acids. These little things unglue the cells and slough them off, leaving clear, smooth skin behind them as they go. The effects are almost immediate, especially if you make them at home, according to my recipes. Before we look at how you can get these spectacular effects at home for a fraction of your child's weekly pocket money (as opposed to the family's weekly food bill, which is the price of some of the AHA creams available in the shops) you need to know two things. First, there is another class of acids, known as the beta hydroxy acids. One of these is called salicylic acid and has been used in wart and acne preparations for some time. This is in its concentrated form. In its natural form it is found in witch hazel. This acid helps the action of the alpha hydroxy acids and we will be utilising it in our recipes. Secondly, AHAs sting. In their concentrated form and even diluted in water they sting. They are acids, after all. Many people think that they cannot use fruit acids for this reason, or perhaps that they must use them only in very diluted concentrations. While I agree with the precaution and advise low concentrations of AHAs, I have found that if you make the pH of your fruit acid preparation more alkaline you will not get the sting. But the preparation will still be very effective. The way to alter the pH is to add borax. It is available from the chemist and costs very little. Now you're ready for some Skin Magic!

DO-IT-YOURSELF FRUIT ACIDS

Simply put a little of your chosen fruit acid in the bottom of a plastic container or glass jar. You can choose either citric acid or tartaric acid. Both are available from any chemist. Handle the raw acid *very* carefully – it could hurt very much if inhaled, if you got it into your eyes or if you swallowed the raw granules. However, your mother probably used it freely when making lemonade, so don't get too worried! By a 'little' I mean about the amount you'd get on the tip of a teaspoon. Add about a third of a teaspoon or less of borax powder. You can overdose on borax through external application, so go easy. At any rate, you'll be using it in small amounts on your face. Borax has been used in cosmetics preparation for centuries. Top up with about 30ml of distilled witch hazel. Put the top on your jar and shake well to dissolve the powdered ingredients. You could add a splash of vegetable glycerine (available from Neal's Yard herb shops and from the Herbal Apothecary) to make the preparations extra gentle. That's it! Easy peasy and incredibly effective. Don't be tempted to increase the concentration of fruit acid in your lotion – you *can* get too much of a good thing – and make sure you don't use this lotion around your eyes. By the way, citric acid is better than tartaric. You could always double the amount of witch hazel if you wish to.

Moisturisers

As you have just seen in the section on Fruit Acids, moisturisers and oils aren't really the answer to dry skin problems. By all means use the Super Oils outlined in the earlier part of this chapter, but to have a real impact on dry, ageing and out-of-condition skin I have a far more exciting approach for you. Instead of oil and moisturiser (which can, if used exclusively, exacerbate dry skin conditions by adding more 'glue' to those unshed cells) think FUNCTION. Your skin is alive, responsive and resilient. It can repair itself. In this section I will show you what to do to return your skin to normal, healthy function. Healthy skin isn't dry and it isn't oily. It's firm and doesn't sag. If you optimise the functioning of your skin, you will produce visible results – beautiful skin.

Some of the oils we met earlier have the capacity to enhance skin function. Oils such as borage, walnut, linseed, evening primrose and the essential oils, especially lavender and lemon. However, too much oil can make your skin puffy, so be aware of that possibility. If you leave a good layer of oil on your skin overnight, you will almost certainly wake up with puffy eyelids. The answer is to tissue off excess and use oils during the day.

In case you need convincing that the *real* benefits and improvements must centre on function and elasticity (which is closely related to good function), try this test. Pick up a make-up mirror and bend over the from the waist. Now look in your mirror. Look at what's happened around your eyes, your mouth, between your eyebrows. Unless you've had cosmetic surgery, you will get a major fright. All that stuff hanging loose out there really *is* your skin and it really *is* that droopy and saggy! Sure, you could have it all cut out, but your basic lack of tone is not changed one little bit by cosmetic surgery. In other words, your skin function *after* surgery is just as awful as before, you just get to ignore it for a bit longer. And eventually ... It all gets too gruesome for words. And I even have a way to frighten those who have succumbed to the knife! This is an even easier test. Simply place your hand flat on the table and relax. Now pinch the skin on the back of your hand gently and pull it up slightly. Let go. How quickly did your skin return from its pinched position? If your skin elasticity is good, it takes a fraction of a second. Maybe one. You'd expect this in a child and in those following the RR programme. An old person's skin might take as long as *five seconds* to return to its original position. An old person on a 'normal' diet, that is. You can improve facial elasticity, at least partially, by doing Face Aerobics. But, as the second test shows you, that's not all there is to it. The rest of you, even your face, will still be marching on towards the Big Sag unless you look at function and elasticity as the prime factors in skin care and beauty.

Here's what you do. Firstly, you begin to eat as much raw food as you can, even all-raw, if at all possible – perhaps one meal a day? Then re-think your skin care. I know that they say you ought to use a sunscreen all the time but somehow that seems too much to me. Some experts have even said that overprotected skin will sag more and be thinner than skin which gets a little bit of gentle sunshine and some sort of stimulation every day. I will talk about this in a minute. For moisturising think elasticity, function and health.

LIQUORICE ROOT

I predict a great future for this root. It has been used internally for centuries in China to prolong life and protect the body. Now even Western scientists have found anti-ageing substances in liquorice root. But as far as elasticity and smooth skin are concerned, this little root is really something! We've already met proteolytic enzymes earlier in this chapter and they are very valuable as mild exfoliating agents which improve skin function, but what liquorice does is something far more exciting. When applied to the skin as a lotion, liquorice root extract has enzyme-altering properties which pretty much immediately means smooth, elastic skin. Used over time the results are remarkable. The enzymes involved in this instance are not digestive enzymes such as the proteolytic enzymes. There are enzymes in the skin which actually act on the collagen itself and destroy it. Liquorice possibly prevents this destruction by altering the activity of those enzymes. This sort of action is a very new and exciting area of cosmetic science.

To make the liquorice root preparation, simply break up a liquorice root or use the pieces of Chinese liquorice root available from herbal suppliers. Use about half a handful of pieces and add one and a half mugs of water. Bring to the boil and simmer for twenty minutes. Leave it to cool and apply to your face at least twice a day. You can, of course, apply it to your neck, hands and elsewhere as you wish. Liquorice powder, by the way, makes a great tooth powder which also tastes nice. And if you have an ulcer, whether in your mouth or in your stomach, liquorice root will heal it. It acts pretty much instantly in the mouth. Liquorice root also prevents tooth decay.

FENNEL SEED

An incredible little dynamo for skin elasticity, fennel contains oestrogen-like compounds and for this reason is not recommended for women with oestrogen-sensitive cancers (the same also applies to liquorice). Many herbalists suggest that fennel is slightly toxic to children under five. It is so widely used in gripe water and toothpaste that the effect must be very slight. However, as far as improving your skin function is concerned, the effect of this herb is wonderful!

To prepare, bruise two large spoonfuls of fennel seeds or use about half that amount in powder form. Add a mugful of water, bring to the boil and then simmer for twenty minutes. Keep the pot covered. Leave to cool and use as above. You can, of course, combine liquorice root and fennel seed in one pot and prepare together to make a fantastic skin lotion for dry and ageing skin. A treatment that really improves the health of your skin. By the way, I don't recommend the use of fennel essential oil as it really is quite powerful.

ALTERNATIVES TO VITASORB C AND VITASORB E

These two preparations are wonderful at improving skin function but if you can't get them, don't worry! Simply use pure, fresh lemon juice as a substitute for VitaSorb C and pure vitamin E as a substitute for VitaSorb E. You could use the vitamin E capsules on sale in health food shops but they are usually mixed with soya oil, making them less useful. The oil is most likely refined and will have the drawbacks I've outlined when using oils. If the lemon juice stings, rinse it off. Keep using it though; you'll find your skin develops a resistance to it as it gets stronger. Of course, being a natural product, you are getting much more than just vitamin C when you use lemon juice. You're getting fruit acids, B vitamins, even some vitamin D. I use lemon juice all the time. I use it on my skin (even around my eyes, but be careful, it can cause redness – if it begins to sting, around the eyes especially, wash it off), on my hair and on my hands. It softens wonderfully, makes skin less red and it gives your complexion a lovely boost which leaves it glowing.

WITCH HAZEL
A very cheap yet incredibly effective face firmer. Use distilled witch hazel all over your face, neck and breasts as often as you remember. It works wonders around the eyes.

VITAMIN B6
This vitamin improves skin function by increasing the synthesis of new collagen. (Avocado does this too.) Don't forget to combine the B6 with other B complex vitamins. Use internally and externally.

CATALASE
Why this is I don't know, but applying a few drops of this enzyme directly to the skin really makes it glow. You'll smell like a goat for a few minutes but the smell goes and the radiance remains! Again, this is not a digestive enzyme. Catalase is responsible for clearing up hydrogen peroxide created when SOD (see pages 86–7) does its anti-oxidant work.

VITASORB A
Do not use vitamin A internally or externally if there is any possibility that you might be pregnant or if you are breast feeding. Otherwise, use two to four drops on your face and neck for a superb firming action. Vitamin A actually thickens and strengthens skin and regular external applications of VitaSorb A produce a visible rejuvenating effect.

BREWER'S YEAST AND BAKER'S YEAST
I've used both and they give you fantastic skin. Brewer's yeast has been shown to contain a skin respiratory factor and baker's yeast has always figured strongly in the quest for great skin. Simply mix to a paste with water and apply to the skin. Rinse off before it has had time to dry.

FRICTION MASSAGE

I don't believe in hurting the skin, but neither do I believe that skin should be pampered and not treated like the alive, resilient organ that it is. You know by now that the way to a beautiful body is not via the sofa. For beautiful skin you also need some action! One method is the Friction Rub. It's very simple. Find an area on your face which you would like to firm up (this shouldn't be too difficult), tense the muscles underlying it and rub. Rub across any wrinkles you wish to eliminate, gently but firmly. Keep moving from one area to the next, always remembering to tense the muscles underneath the area to be treated. Hold firm while you rub. You can oil your face lightly beforehand if you wish. Add lavender oil for an extra-value Friction Rub! Peppermint oil is good too, but strong, so start with low concentrations diluted in a carrier oil. Salt can also be used to enhance the friction effect. Use it over oil to avoid scratching your skin.

KELP

Seaweed, of course, is great for the hair, inside and out, but it's equally good for your skin, enhancing its moistness and good condition. In Brazil, the seaweed pickers noticed a great improvement in the condition and elasticity of their skin when they began handling seaweed regularly. The easiest way to gain benefits for your face (and body) is simply to rub kelp powder, slightly moistened, over your face and body. It will improve the glow and function of your skin.

SKIN POLISHER

This is a fantastic preparation for the days when you need *instant help*. Even the first application should produce an appreciable softening of your skin. You can feel it nourishing your tired, thirsty and hungry cells.

To make it, simply pour half a cup of walnut oil (or linseed or hazelnut) into the blender jug, add a heaped teaspoon of lecithin granules and a third cup each of distilled witch hazel and rosewater. Blend well at high speed. You should get a lovely white lotion. Store in the fridge if possible. Use as often as you like. This preparation will not leave your skin puffy, even around your eyes.

WHAT TO DO ABOUT WRINKLES AND OTHER DISASTERS

When you're young it's spots, when you're older it's wrinkles – a new one always appears just when you thought life was perfect. So here are ways to show you that even if life isn't, your face and body can be (pretty damn close, anyway).

Wrinkles First

Take organic sulphur (two), Spectrumzyme (three first thing and three with each meal), a good B complex (one), a multivitamin and multimineral (one), vitamin C (half a teaspoon of powder or 1500 mg), zinc citrate (about 7 mg) and vitamin E (300 i.u.) each day. Apply VitaSorb C at least twice daily over your face, including around the eyes. Add VitaSorb E each evening. Use the zinc oxide powder and walnut oil mix as a sunscreen every day. Definitely no animal products of any sort (take B12 and Full Spectrum Amino Acids) and follow the RR Diet. This approach yields *visible* results from day one in most people. If you follow this regime for six months you will be astonished at the degree of rejuvenation which is possible. With the above protocol, even Face Aerobics become optional rather than necessary. Make sure you aren't doing *anything* – including exercises – that may be creating new lines or deepening existing ones. Exercises for the eye area and the forehead and frown lines which are sometime suggested in books and magazines can produce or deepen lines. You can be trying to get rid of horizontal lines on the forehead and at the same time deepening your frown lines and vice versa. So be careful and watch out for this possibility.

What to Do if You Tend to Wake up with Puffy Eyes and a Creased Face

You need to take some liver and kidney tonics. Try barberry and turmeric in combination, or yellow dock. Dandelion root (unroasted) is also good but can be too mild for stubborn cases. Make it a part of your everyday diet – simply chew a piece of the root every day (delicious if it's of good quality). Barberry and turmeric are best brewed up together – bring a teaspoon of each and three mugfuls of water to the boil and simmer for twenty minutes. Drink warm, not hot, three times daily. At the beginning of the programme it's fine to use these decoctions and teas made from medicinal herbs. Later, when you are sorted out, you will probably find that you don't need them and prefer to use the herbs in their raw, powdered form. A good kidney tonic is one handful of Gou Qi Zi berries each day. You will find more information on these wonder-workers in the chapter on herbs. The RR Diet is, again, very important. Use VitaSorb C every night, at bed-time. All over your face. You will wake up with a younger face!

What to Do about Lines around the Mouth

These may be a result of smoking. If this is the case, the first part of the answer is obvious. Apply VitaSorb C and VitaSorb E around and on the mouth twice daily. Coupled with the RR Diet, a multivit/mineral, Organic Sulphur, Vitamin C, beta carotene and Full Spectrum Amino Acids, you should see an improvement within four months.

What to Do about Sallow, Dull Skin

This skin is starved of oxygen. To improve circulation apply VitaSorb E and lavender oil. Sometimes I use the oil neat but it is very strong that way. Dilute it in jojoba oil. Add rosemary oil to really rev up that circulation! Take Iron EAP2 at suppertime with a little vitamin C powder and eat spirulina or chlorella. Use enzymes (such as Spectrumzyme) instead of soap when you wash your face. Use borage oil at least twice each day on your face (morning and evening). It increases cell oxygenation very effectively. Soon your skin will be pink and glowing!

How to Have Firm, Soft Skin

Here is a good little programme for external skin care. You'll be pleasantly amazed what a difference it can make to the look and feel of your skin and FAST. It's very easy – first wet your face with warm water. In fact, whatever you use to moisturise your face, try it on top of wet skin – the results are better. Follow this with an application of one of these oils: walnut, borage, hazelnut, jojoba, extra virgin olive or evening primrose. Then apply some fresh juice; lemon works very well but so does red grape or orange. Finally, take some good sea salt (Celtic sea salt is best) and gently rub it all over your face. Rinse with warm water and finish with an application of distilled witch hazel (available from chemists) which you just leave to dry on your face. Witch hazel is a much neglected face firmer; regular use really does tone your face. I've even seen it firm up varicose veins. This whole programme is actually quite quick to do but it does everything you want (except provide a sunscreen and that doesn't matter – just treat it as a cleansing programme and apply the sunscreen after the witch hazel if you are going out afterwards). It moisturises, stimulates the circulation, exfoliates and tones. So make it one of your better habits!

In this chapter you found many recommendations for supplement programmes suitable for specific problems. They will work whatever diet you're on (within reason – a very bad diet is a big problem for your body and even supplements will have a hard job trying to help you. 'Bad' is: sugar, white flour, meat, alcohol, you know the sort of thing. For more about diet see Part Three). But they will work *spectacularly* well with the Radical Rejuvenation Diet. You will also find suggestions on doses, such as 'one capsule'. I am using this as a unit of measurement – I do not suggest that you actually consume the gelatine or even vegetable-derived capsule in which your supplement is packaged. Always pour the contents out of the capsule and mix with water, fresh juice, bananas, fruit mix or whatever you can invent to disguise the taste. The taste is not nearly as fabulous as the results. So what? In my experience good taste leads to spots and cellulite. Though that's completely unfair to the delicious tastes you can create on the Radical Rejuvenation Diet, as you will see in Part Three.

CHAPTER TWO

Remake Your Hair

Hair can be a real headache. It grows luxuriantly in all the wrong places (armpits, calves) and then hardly at all where it should. But even if your most luxurious growth is in unmentionable places and you can count the stuff on your head without the aid of machines, there is hope. More than that, even. Here is a practical programme which works. You can have thicker hair very soon.

First of all a little information. Hair loves minerals. It loves good nutrition generally, but it *especially* loves minerals. It goes for hard-to-get-ones in a big way – silica, sulphur and iodine. But it also likes the more common zinc, iron and calcium and, of course, our 'normal' Western diet is almost impressively deficient in minerals. You name it, it's deficient in it and hair notices. It splits and breaks and thins and refuses to grow. Until it gets those minerals. That's the only way to get it to behave. The only way to radically improve your hair is to give it what it needs.

WHAT YOUR HAIR REALLY NEEDS
Sulphur

The gypsies knew – they used to make a hair-growing tonic by macerating one chopped-up onion in some brandy, letting it steep for two weeks and using it as a daily hair rub after straining off the onion pieces. Onion contains a good supply of sulphur. As does garlic. It has also been used externally to promote hair growth. But hair seems to like Organic Sulphur from BioScience best of all. You may have to obtain it through a nutritional practitioner or from the Nutri Centre (BioScience sells only to practitioners). It's worth the effort. After three months or so you will have heavy, thick, healthy hair and not a split end in sight.

Another way of increasing hair thickness and strength is to take cysteine. Cysteine is an amino acid which contains sulphur and which has a special affinity for the hair. Take it, as all aminos, on an empty stomach, with a capsule of B complex and one of Magnesium EAP2, at least half an hour before food. The product I recommend is Amino-Plex from BioCare, which also contains two other amino acids: another sulphur-containing amino, the liver protector methionine, as well as lysine, which has been used to lessen attacks of genital herpes. The combination of all these amino acids will also aid the functioning of the GLA (gamma linolenic acid pathway) which is more good news for your hair and skin.

Silica

Horsetail and nettle leaves both contain silica and, taken internally as well as applied as external hair tonics, they will produce a remarkably shiny head of hair. Ask a horse breeder. They add these herbs to their horse's feed precisely because it gives the animal's coat such a stunning shine. Pity they don't eat the feed themselves. Their own hair could use some, too. You can obtain these herbs from herbal suppliers in powdered form. Do not use tinctures for internal use in this case, as the silica content will be low. If you choose horsetail powder (*Equisetum arvense*), combine it with an equal amount of marshmallow root powder (one teaspoon). Dried nettle doesn't sting, by the way. It is safe for internal use.

Other Minerals ... Zinc, Iron, Iodine and Calcium

Make friends with seaweed. The dried sort which has not been cooked. Soak it in water or eat it out of the packet in the case of dulse. My kids love it and everyone knows children will *never* eat anything just because it's good for them. Seaweed takes a few months to sort your hair out. But even if your hair is good, you should get friendly with seaweed. It contains just the right blend of minerals to build a healthy body.

Because we are all constantly taking 'supplements' of lead, pesticides, even carbon tetrachloride on occasion, and many other frankly poisonous substances, our bodies cannot derive everything they need for superb health from food. A partially poisoned body needs a big helping hand. This is why it is so important to add powerful concentrated supplements to any health programme. Many of these will even detoxify your body from toxic substances lodged in your body tissues. So do not ignore the supplements; you need them even if you are eating the best diet in the world. Which is a diet consisting of raw foods only.

Iron-depleted hair is thin, weak and feeble and falls out by the handful. If you have recently given birth and resumed your periods, you know what I mean. Take Iron EAP2 from BioCare. It will not cause stomach upsets and it is a superbly well absorbed product. If you are taking vitamin E, which, by the way, is also very good for hair, leave at least twelve hours between iron and the E vitamin – iron destroys vitamin E. However, I don't think this is such a real problem when using products from BioCare, as they are so quickly assimilated by the body. But just to be safe and to ensure complete assimilation, take your vitamin E with breakfast and your iron with supper.

Similarly, zinc has been found to be best absorbed when taken without food at bedtime. If you use zinc citrate you will find quite rapid effects as it is very well absorbed; better sleep, smoother skin, stronger nails and hair.

Calcium EAP2 and potassium iodide (the latter found in the multivit/mineral combination and both produced by BioCare) are well tolerated and assimilated very efficiently by the body. They will strengthen the structure of your hair. In addition, calcium is important for the repair of varicose veins.

Protein

Hair is made of keratin, which is a protein, and the best way to make new, strong keratin is to supply your body with plenty of utilisable amino acids, so make sure you include Full Spectrum Aminos in your daily diet. The best ones have been described in the chapter on skin.

Vitamins

A lack of vitamin E leads to thin hair. Taking the vitamin internally helps, of course, but I love plastering it on to my hair and scalp. B complex is terrific for your hair, too. It makes another highly effective hair conditioner when used externally. For more ideas on using vitamins as edible, effective and inexpensive external hair treatments, see the suggestions on external treats below.

EXTERNAL TREATS FOR YOUR HAIR

Recently my hair suddenly became blonder. I hadn't had it bleached or dyed; I simply switched my shampoo. I stopped using commercial, detergent-based products and began using a very-easy-to-make recipe which I invented myself based on what is known about the biological needs of hair. Commercial shampoos are tinned food for your hair. The shampoo which you can make yourself in minutes if you follow my instructions is more like a vitamin pill. Don't be alarmed by the oils and vitamins and other substances which I suggest for use on the hair; they may *seem* crude and simple and unglamorous but their effects are not. Okay, so your hair might have to look oily for a while sometimes before you wash it. Enjoy it; you're feeding your starved locks! And when you wash the treatment off you'll be left with what you want – stronger, healthier, thicker hair.

You can thicken and strengthen your hair in minutes by applying flowers of sulphur directly to it, like a pack – you'll need to mix the flowers of sulphur with something like fuller's earth in a blender with some water to a paste consistency, as flowers of sulphur is a powder which does not dissolve in water. I often use this as a shampoo by itself and it is a remarkable body builder for hair. Unfortunately you can't use it if you have used any kind of chemical on your hair, or even if you've used vegetable colour on it – the sulphur can react with any of these agents to produce a rather startling green colour. On untreated hair it's fine. You do need to rinse and rinse, though, as this paste is rather heavy and thick.

There is a more expensive way of getting sulphur to your hair quickly and the cost is this method's *only* disadvantage. So if you can, use this method in preference to the one described above. In fact, you only need to use small amounts of this product, so it does work out pretty well on the cost side, too. The product in question is BioScience Organic Sulphur. It will *not* colour or in any way adversely affect your hair so you can use it to repair chemically damaged locks without fear. Organic Sulphur (methylsulphonyl-methane or MSM) is a source of sulphur which is highly active biologically and can be taken internally as well to greatly improve the strength, thickness and health of your hair (see earlier). And the way to use it as a quick hair restorer is simply to empty one capsule of Organic Sulphur into a cup, add a little water, stir to dissolve and apply to your hair. You can use it when your hair is dry or on wet hair, following your wash. It will make a great difference to both the strength and the softness of your hair, which will feel heavier and look shinier even after one application. What I like about this approach (of using products which are very bio-available and beneficial whether used internally or externally) is that the beauty treatment is also a heath treatment, providing your hair with real building blocks – something it actually *needs* for good health. So the conditioning effect is not only cosmetic and is not temporary. Regular applications make your hair healthier and stronger.

TREATMENT SHAMPOOS

A good shampoo can be made by soaking a handful of split, red lentils in a bowl with plenty of water so that all the lentils are well covered. Leave overnight and in the morning blend thoroughly in the blender. Strain very well, using a piece of muslin and a sieve. You can keep it in the fridge for a few days. It makes a very good, strengthening and thickening shampoo and it's lovely and pink.

A great way to lighten, soften and condition dingy hair is to make a shampoo from psyllium seed husks (fine grade) and lemons. Psyllium lightens hair even by itself, but here the effect is magnified by the addition of a lemon. Psyllium is a much beloved substance in our house on account of its ability to make an instant, gooey gel when mixed with hot water. Depending on the amount of water added, it can be merely sticky and stretchy, or, with much more of the powder in proportion to the liquid, it makes an outer space glop according to my children and it leaves your hair very soft, too. For this purpose, however, make the psyllium preparation quite dilute and mix it with some well cooked, sliced lemon (including peel and pips). Include the cooking water from the lemon, but make sure all the liquids are *cool*, not hot, when mixing with the psyllium. Whiz it all up in the blender and you have a lovely cream shampoo for depressed hair. Your hair will feel thick, heavy, healthy and soft after this shampoo. If your hair is mousy, dark blonde or even dark and dull, the psyllium and lemon treatment will bring out lovely blonde highlights. Just to be safe, do a strand test before using it on chemically treated hair but it should be fine. Always use cool, never hot, water to prepare psyllium products. Brush hair well when dry. Psyllium gel also makes a nice, conditioning face wash.

The Best Shampoo in the World

I have tried lots of shampoos; home-made, shop-bought, vegan, vegetarian and animal. Now, of course, I would not use animal-derived products, that is, ones containing hydrolysed animal protein. Also, I have found that natural products, whether in shampoos or creams, really don't work as well when they are combined with chemical emulsifiers, preservatives and colouring. So, as I said, I've tried *lots* of ways to wash my hair. For a long time my hair looked awful because I just couldn't find anything that really worked. And then I found it. Here it is. The Best Shampoo in the World. It contains lecithin, B vitamins, iron, cysteine and all of the amino acids essential for humans. It's raw and *very* effective. You will never need to use anything else on your hair again. It conditions your locks as it cleans. There are even reports of regular use encouraging healthy, thick hair growth. And to top it all it's incredibly simple to make and use. Just whip up two or three (depending on hair length) egg yolks, wet your hair and then use them as your shampoo. I don't recommend using the whites because they have a drying effect. With the yolks, too, you don't have to worry about scrambling the eggs on your head. Still, don't use very hot water just to be on the safe side!

You will find more ideas to clean your hair, face and even teeth without the use of harmful detergents in the chapter on lifestyle.

Hair Shine

When you use the above shampoo your hair will be soft, glossy and lovely. However, like everyone else, I'm always trying out new things. This one's very easy to make and very inexpensive, yet it gives your hair a really pro-gloss. Just mix a small amount (about half a teaspoon or less) of glycerine (get vegetable glycerine if you can) with half a cup of rose water or a rose water and witch hazel mixture. You can use this on your hair when it's dry or wet. If you're using it on dry rather than wet hair, comb it through to the ends, wait until it dries then brush well. Your hair will be gorgeous! Vegetable glycerine is available from Neal's Yard Apothecary or the Herbal Apothecary.

Hair Polisher

This is exactly the same preparation as the Skin Polisher on page 44. Wet your hair, apply a little of the polisher to your hair and leave on for as long as you wish. You could cover your whole head with a towel turban to stop cold drips running down your neck. When you're ready, use the egg yolk shampoo described above to wash out the polisher. Use two or even three washes.

STIMULATING HAIR TREATMENT

This very unlikely treatment makes your hair *wonderful*! It's based on the very ancient method of healing which uses water to stimulate cell function. And it works! Try it – it's free and easy and effective. This is what you do: just before bedtime (you could do this any time, of course, but before bed is the best time, unusually, as you can leave the treatment working for the desired time), fill a sink with cold water from the tap and immerse your head in it. Make sure that you can feel the cold all over the scalp. Each area should receive about ten to thirty seconds of cold water therapy. Then blot off excess water with a towel and, if your hair is long, twist it up on top of your head.

Finally cover your head with a woolly hat. I use an acrylic one but a woolly one would be even better. That's it! Leave the hat on until your hair is dry, which generally means about eight hours (hence the recommendation for an all-night treatment). But if you can only manage thirty minutes or so, do that instead. You will find that your scalp quickly warms up and feels wonderful – glowing and alive. This treatment stimulates hair growth and makes your hair soft and bouncy.

OTHER FAVOURITE TREATS
Jojoba Oil

This is a wonderful liquid wax which is really easily absorbed by the hair (and skin) without making it horribly greasy. One of the best pre-shampoo conditioners ever. Don't forget to use two or three washes following an oil pre-treatment to leave your hair really clean and shiny.

Blue-green Algae

I've never seen anything else quite like this – not as far as shiny, soft hair is concerned, anyway. Chlorella and sisters spirulina and Lake Klamath algae can make your hair shinier and softer pretty much overnight. Just eat some every day.

Not long ago, my daughter's hair, which was weak and thin, just wouldn't grow. It had remained somewhere just past her shoulders for what seemed like years. This is what I gave her:

One part spirulina powder
One part horsetail powder
Two parts alfalfa powder
One part rosehip powder
Two parts nettle powder

The 'parts' way of measuring is really easy: if you're using teaspoons then one part equals one teaspoon, two parts equals two teaspoons and so on. You can use any measure to represent one part as long as you are consistent throughout the recipe. How big your measure is depends on how much mixture you want to make. My daughter took a large spoonful of the mixture in water every morning. Within two weeks her hair was stronger and less than two months later the longest bits were brushing her waist! It has also acquired a superb sheen and has turned blonder than ever.

Another good thing to do if your hair is unwell is to give it a four-week B complex course. Simply take a high dose of a very good B complex each day for four weeks, then reduce it to a maintenance dose. A high dose is anything above 100 mg. I recommend 150 mg of each of the major B vitamins, at the end of the course gradually reducing it over two weeks to 25 mg. You can repeat this two or three times a year. You will notice a big improvement in the condition of your scalp, hair and skin.

Vitamin C

BioCare make two products containing a suitable form of vitamin C; one is called Vitasorb C and the other is Derma C. I have found Vitasorb C to be much better for skin application, tightening eyelids, removing lines and wrinkles and so on, while Derma C works better on hair. You can use it before a wash or after you've washed your hair, while it's still wet. You needn't rinse it off. The vitamin C leaves your hair silky, just like in all the best adverts. You could even dissolve a B complex or a multivit/mineral in water and use it as a rinse-out conditioner. Your hair will be pleased.

Essential Oils

The best oil for thin hair is cedarwood. I use it neat, straight out of the bottle. Rub two or three drops into your scalp and enjoy the scent. Rosemary is also good but dilute it in a little vegetable oil – a light one is best; safflower, sesame, walnut, hazelnut or sunflower are all good. You will probably want to use this as a pre-shampoo treatment because it will be oily. Or you can add a few drops of rosemary oil to a small bottle filled with water. Shake well and rub into the scalp. Keep it in the fridge and shake before each use.

Movement Therapy

It sounds mad, I know, but tugging and pulling your hair is great for your scalp. It's a bit like hair jogging, really. Bend over from the waist and grab handfuls of hair close to the scalp; pull it and make little circles with it and whatever else tickles your fancy. Don't be vicious but don't be shy, either. You ought to *feel* something! And one day it will feel good, suddenly. All that lovely oxygen getting to that tired scalp.

WHAT TO DO ABOUT HAIR PROBLEMS
What to Do about Greying Hair

The most important thing is to take He Shou Wu every day. About one teaspoonful of the powder or the tincture each day is sufficient to bring your original colour back. I've seen it happen and so have others who have used this wonderful plant in therapy. Allow *at least* three months for visible results, maybe more. But, when you think about it, even three months isn't all that long! Make sure also that your diet is supremely well supplied with B vitamins. I would recommend BioCare's Enzyme activated B complex in this case. The B vitamin PABA (or para-amino-benzoic acid) has also successfully restored grey hair to its original colour. However, don't take any B vitamins in isolation. Always take the whole complex. He Shou Wu is my favourite for grey hair, though. Also take Organic Sulphur, powdered alfalfa herb and dried, powdered nettle internally. They are all magnificent hair restorers and tonics.

What to Do if Your Hair Won't Grow

Here we're talking iron, vitamin E, amino acids, spirulina, Lake Klamath algae or chlorella and the super-hair-strengthener Organic Sulphur. Take one Iron EAP2, 200 i.u. of vitamin E (that's four drops of VitaSorb E) and one teaspoonful of Full Spectrum Amino Acid powder with each meal and at least twelve tablets of chlorella (about 3 grams) or the equivalent of spirulina or Lake Klamath algae and a capsule of Organic Sulphur each day. Take everything with breakfast except for the iron. Take that at suppertime.

What to Do about Thin Hair

Take two capsules of Organic Sulphur at breakfast, a teaspoon of amino acid powder at each meal, and use a sulphur hair strengthener. Use either flowers of sulphur or Organic Sulphur dissolved in water applied to wet hair. Organic Sulphur can also be used on dry hair between shampoos. Use the red lentil hair shampoo described in this chapter and eat seaweed!

What to Do about Dull, Lifeless Hair

You need dried alfalfa and chlorella, Lake Klamath algae or spirulina. Take about one teaspoon of each. That's the minimum dose. Also take one large spoonful of walnut oil, a good B complex and a multi-vitamin/mineral. And rub some Derma C cream into your hair while it's still wet from washing.

What to Do if Your Hair Is Very Dry and Tangles Easily

Tangled hair can be caused by a deficiency of biotin, a vitamin of the B Complex group, which has recently been cropping up in some hair care products, together with its brother, pantothenic acid or panto-thenate. To supply your hair with both these hair essentials, take a B complex, one capsule with breakfast. Tangling is also caused by a deficiency of essential fatty acids, particularly of the Omega 3 type, so take a tablespoon of walnut oil each morning together with half a teaspoon or about three capsules of normal strength evening primrose oil to supply GLA (gamma linolenic acid) for the proper functioning of the Omega 6 fatty acid cycle.

CHAPTER THREE

How to Have a Sexy Body

Some people's bodies are like sacks of flour – stodgy, heavy and asleep. I think intelligence is sexy. I think energy is sexy. Muscles are sexy. Not huge and overworked, though. Lean and well defined, firm and juicy is sexy.

Your body can become refined enough to exhibit awareness,

aliveness and intelligence. You can have young legs. You can have a flat stomach, firm breasts and a tight behind. Not that long ago and before RR, I had coming-on-forty legs. They weren't bad. But, my goodness, they weren't anything like the legs I've got now. It's simple. You can do it, too. Just follow the arrows. A bit like science really, or cookery. You can refine your body to the point of intelligence and beauty.

CARNITINE

Success and failure can both be difficult to handle at times. I've had people stop taking carnitine or lowering the dose after only a few days because the weight was dropping off so fast and they were beginning to look so much better than they were used to. But looking great is not so bad and you can get used to everything – even being beautiful. Here's your chance to prove it. Just take one capsule of carnitine (make sure it is L-carnitine), an amino acid, on an empty stomach with a good B complex and some magnesium. Do not eat for one hour afterwards. You may find that morning is the most convenient time to do this. It is also the time I suggest – your energy may well increase so much after you've taken this little trio that you might not want to sleep for hours! Which may or may not be a good thing! The doses you want are: 200 mg for L-carnitine, a B complex which supplies 25 mg of the major B vitamins and 50–100 mg of magnesium. That's on top of your usual magnesium and B complex. L-carnitine is also good for your heart. But what will really get you smiling is the way it gets your cells to convert fat to energy. It's an incredibly good arrangement. Carnitine supplements are derived from beef. If you wish to use an alternative, go for ginseng, pollen and/or royal jelly. You will find information on ginseng in the chapter on herbs and details on pollen and royal jelly in the chapter entitled 'Diet and Lifestyle'. Or you can take the amino acids lysine and methionine which your body uses to make its own carnitine. Don't forget to take them with plenty of water, B complex and magnesium. Amino-Plex from BioCare will supply useful amounts of lysine, methionine and cysteine.

ENZYMES

If you want to look young and lithe, enzymes will get you there. They have been used therapeutically for many conditions, including cancers, allergies and wound healing – even the healing of surgical incisions. Everyone who has used them has a high opinion of them. Especially me. I love enzymes. You can even use them to get rid of stuffed-up noses. But we're interested in something much less prosaic – getting rid of ageing! For that, you need to change your diet, too, of course. Take three enzyme capsules when you first get up in the morning, then the same dose with every meal. Stir the powder into water and drink. Not only will you derive much more energy from your food than you normally do; your skin will begin to look younger and more elastic. For an even greater effect, take the Spectrumzyme on an empty stomach each time and leave a gap of twenty minutes before you eat. It's fine to combine Spectrumzyme and L-carnitine first thing if you wish to try them both.

FULL SPECTRUM AMINO ACIDS

We've already met these in the chapters on skin and hair but I have to mention them again because just one week's worth of therapy using these little dynamos can produce visible, firm muscles in your legs and arms. Nothing too showy – just sexy limbs, that's all. Take one teaspoon of the powder with every meal. I prefer the powder because you get more that way even though it looks more expensive when you're standing at the till. I also like it when I decide my own needs and quantities, which is easier with a tub full of powder than a container of capsules.

MULTIVITAMIN AND MULTIMINERAL COMPLEX

Obvious, but easily forgotten, and don't leave out the walnut and evening primrose oil. Fat may not be good, but these oils definitely are. Fat from animal sources is fattening. Oils from walnuts and hazelnuts, borage and evening primrose seeds are youth enhancing. I hope you're on your way to the health food shop. Supermarket oils are often not cold-pressed and may be refined, so be careful.

SKIN BRUSHING

Everybody loves this one – why all that modified scratching should feel so good, I don't know, but it does and it cleanses and stimulates your lymphatic system and tones your body to boot. A long-handled bristle brush is best. Begin by stroking (not too hard or it really will be 'scratching') from your foot to your knee several times, then from the knee to the hip. Repeat with your other leg. Then do circles on your tummy and *gentle* circles on your breasts. Then up your arms from wrists to shoulder, down your back as best as you can and up your bottom. Do it for as long as it feels good. Aim for every day, except that it doesn't always work out quite like that, so do it when you remember. It's a good idea to do it before a bath so that you can wash off all that grime. Remember *never* to brush varicose veins.

COLD BATHS

This one *never* gets any easier, even in the middle of a heat wave. But a mistress of a French king was a dedicated cold bather and kept him interested well into her old age and Paul Newman's got his own version (he dunks his head into a bucket of ice-cold water) and he looks nearly as good so there's no point arguing. It does firm up the body and certainly wakes you up. Too much, sometimes. It also stimulates your inner organs and immunity and tones and tightens all the bits you manage to submerge for more than a second. Which isn't easy, especially at first. But there is something very subtle at work here (as with all techniques which lead to greater vitality) – your body loves it even if you hate it and once your body has experienced the benefits of cold baths, it will get you there even as you're coming up with some great excuses to get out of there!

Cold baths are very simple on paper – just fill a tub to about four or six inches with water from the cold tap and get in. It will be standing only for a few days, then (gingerly) perhaps a little sit down. Later you might try lying down on your back briefly and on your front. Just think how firm your breasts will be and try it for more than two seconds. Something like ten seconds working up to sixty and perhaps going for three minutes, one day. It will take three months or so of gradual daily acclimatisation to reach the longer times. The greatest benefits from this technique come after prolonged use. More than three months, at least. Your immune system should be pretty well revved up by then and – don't yawn – the immune system is vital to youthfulness. And if your colleagues should find you a little too energetic and cheerful in the mornings after your splash (morning is the best time), tell them to jump into a cold bath themselves. By the way, when the weather is very cold, do add some hot water to your cold bath – just enough to take the vicious edge off!

WHAT TO DO ABOUT VARICOSE VEINS

Eat a good, raw food diet or a mostly raw food diet. Exclude all animal products. This is important because both the protein and the saturated fat found in animal products have a detrimental effect on varicose veins. Also exclude bread. If you are choosing to eat some cooked foods, use brown rice and baked potatoes instead of bread as your source of complex carbohydrates. Take BioCare Calcium EAP2 (two capsules), BioCare Magnesium EAP2 (two capsules), Organic Sulphur (two capsules, made by BioScience) and 400 i.u. of vitamin E. If you are using VitaSorb E from BioCare, 400 i.u. means eight drops – work up to this dose by starting with 100 i.u. (two drops) and adding 50 i.u. (one drop) each week until you reach the target level of 400 i.u. This is a safe level to keep up for several months. When you wish to decrease it, take it down again in 50 i.u. steps over a few weeks. Also take one teaspoon of horsetail powder (*Equisetum arvense*) and one teaspoon of marshmallow root powder. Blueberry extract has been found to be remarkably effective and safe in strengthening and healing varicose veins – if you can't find the extract, eat lots of the fresh berries whenever you get the chance.

VitaSorb C, applied externally to the veins and surrounding tissues, has produced some remarkable effects – it strengthens the connective tissue and the blood vessels and the whole treated area begins to look healthier after as little as two weeks of daily application. Distilled witch hazel has a firming effect, too.

HOW TO HAVE INVITING, SEXY EYES

If your eyes are often red, you need to increase your intake of B complex vitamins. Take one capsule of B complex each day with breakfast or lunch. If you take it with supper you may find that you are too energetic to sleep! Also concentrate on taking care of your liver. (Ever noticed how red your eyes get when you've been drinking? That's your liver talking.) The best protectors for your liver are: the amino acid methionine, which even protects against paracetamol poisoning, and milk thistle seed. Take one capsule of methionine on an empty stomach half an hour before breakfast together with a capsule of B complex and one capsule of Magnesium EAP2. Take one teaspoon of milk thistle powder or the contents of three to six capsules each day. Also take Gou Qi Zi berries, one handful per day. Nothing brightens your eyes faster than Gou Qi Zi. And they taste good and give you lots of energy, too! Sparkling, clear eyes and lots of energy are a pretty sexy combination, so don't neglect this bit!

HOW TO HAVE A FLAT STOMACH

Take hot barberry and turmeric 'tea' three times a day for one week (for recipe see page 28). Take three Spectrumzymes with each meal and 200–250 mg of L-carnitine (plus one BioCare B complex and one BioCare Magnesium EAP2) on an empty stomach half an hour before breakfast. Rub liberal amounts of VitaSorb C (it's cheap enough, thank goodness!) on to your stomach at least twice a day. Be careful, though, it is slightly yellow and sticky so protect your clothing. Take three BioScience Organic Sulphur capsules each morning and one teaspoon of horsetail powder with one teaspoon marshmallow root powder. No animal products and no saturated fats of any sort (not even coconut or palm oil which contain saturated fats, too).

HOW TO MEND SAGGY SKIN ANYWHERE ON THE BODY

Eliminate animal products from your diet completely. Take three BioScience Organic Sulphur capsules in the morning and two in the evening. Take one teaspoon of horsetail powder and one teaspoon of marshmallow root powder, half a teaspoon of vitamin C powder with breakfast and half a teaspoon with supper and half a tablet of BioCare zinc citrate at bedtime at least half an hour after eating. This gives you 7 mg of elemental zinc – if you can't get hold of the product from BioCare, try Solgar or other companies and take the equivalent dose.

HOW TO MEND SAGGY BREASTS

At breakfast take three capsules of BioScience Organic Sulphur each morning and one teaspoon of horsetail powder with one teaspoon of marshmallow root powder, one capsule of BioCare Calcium EAP2 and one capsule of Magnesium EAP2. Take half a tablet of zinc citrate at bedtime. Rub tincture of myrrh, distilled witch hazel (both available from chemists) and BioCare VitaSorb C into the breasts twice a day. Protect clothing from the yellow VitaSorb C and tincture of myrrh.

WHAT TO DO ABOUT ROUGH PATCHES ON UPPER THIGHS AND ARMS

Take two tablespoons of walnut oil with breakfast every day and one capsule of Magnesium EAP2. Take half a tablet (7 mg of elemental zinc) of zinc citrate at bedtime, on an empty stomach. Make sure you eat at least two large salads a day; better still, follow the RR Diet.

CHAPTER FOUR

How to Be Great in Bed

This one's my favourite. As long as you're doing it, it seems, Eternity's interested. Sexy people look younger longer. Aphrodisiacs make great tonics – they balance your hormones and make you smile. They can even make you stand straight and walk tall which ought to please your mother. Of course, it's trendy to be sceptical and sceptical's easy. Try open minded for a while. I've seen these things at work. This chapter is not long but it is effective. The results may surprise you.

ROXY'S FAVOURITE APHRODISIACS

Histidine

The reason they said 'diamonds are a girl's best friend' is because they hadn't heard of histidine. You might exhaust your man but he'll be smiling. Give him Ashwagandha – which gives him the sex drive and strength of a stallion. He'll need all the Ashwagandha he can get with you on histidine. Some people suggest that men should not take histidine but my own informal investigations have produced some very interesting results. However, if your man suffers from premature ejaculation, he ought to take methionine instead.

Catuaba

This one's hot. Probably the world's most uncivilised supplement! And anything that makes you feel that good is going to make you look pretty fantastic. Don't just try it, buy a sackful. And don't believe all those boring grown-ups who say pompous things such as, 'Of course, it's only natural that the sex drive diminishes with age.' Not true! It does happen but it doesn't *have* to. I've never met anyone who really WANTS it to happen. So get some Catuaba, it's Brazilian!

Good health is an absolute must for great sex – booze and fags don't really get you there – you look and smell too awful, for a start. Cigarettes are wrinkles in expensive packets.

Some aphrodisiacs have effects which show up only during lovemaking (histidine, for instance). But some increase and enhance all of your sensual awareness so that you feel more turned on to the whole world all day long (and at night-time, too!). Their action is less specific and more tonifying, balancing and vitalising. Ginseng, Schizandra and Dang Gui are some of the best. In the more specific category I would also include Muira Puama which has recently begun surprising people.

Muira Puama

Well, it is a little surprising to take a spoonful of muddy looking, *unpromising* looking powder, stir it into some water, drink and – turn into a wild animal! This one's also Brazilian. If you want fireworks, get some. I rate it way up there with Catuaba, Ashwagandha and histidine. Its Latin name is *Liriosma ovata* and it is only just becoming famous but Herbal Apothecary stock it. It works brilliantly well in powder form. It does wild things to both men and women. Its method of action is as yet unknown, which doesn't matter that much. It's safe in normal doses, for instance, one large spoonful per day, so you can go and conduct your own scientific experiments. Field study, it's called. Who knows, this time it really might be!

Niacin

This is a form of vitamin B3, which also comes in the form of niacinamide, nicotinamide and nicotinic acid. The niacin form is interesting for lovers. You need to take a tablet containing at least 100 mg of niacin and chew it. It tastes terrible, of course. But it's more effective when you chew it. Why is it that so many things which are good for you taste so bad? Come to think of it, lots of things taste bad – even the ones which are bad for you. So there you are. I do like philosophy. You will soon experience the 'niacin flush' – your ears will burn and turn red, your face will feel hot, even your knees will feel hot and red and tingly. Some people's noses run. Sounds fun? Read on. Because this response is connected with the release of histamine and is linked with mediating the sexual response. Eating niacin makes more than just your knees feel hot! And it lasts past the red and tingly stage, which is over in about half an hour. Some people really don't like it, some (like myself) like it a lot. It's harmless but if you suffer from hay fever, asthma, eczema or any other allergy, use some of the other aphrodisiacs described in this chapter. The vitamin company called Quest make a vitamin B complex which contains niacin. It's always a good idea, even when concentrating on one particular vitamin, such as niacin here, to take it together with the whole B complex. Niacin has been used in large doses (as much as three grams daily) to detoxify alcoholics and drug addicts. Niacin and histidine both work by releasing histamine from the mast cells. If you don't like the idea of the 'niacin flush', simply use histidine. It works very well and does not produce flushing. There have been reports recently of niacin causing liver damage. This happens with large daily doses (over two grams per day) used without the whole B complex and is not a common side effect by any means. In fact, Dr Abram Hoffer has been using such doses with elderly people for many years as a means of reversing ageing and has had very good results indeed. The dose of 100 mg recommended here is obviously much lower, and, at any rate, is recommended as an occasional stimulant rather than prolonged treatment. For long-term treatment, chose histidine, Catuaba or Muira Puama.

Ginseng

No book on rejuvenation would be complete without ginseng. Once it was worth more than its weight in gold and wars were fought over it. Nowadays you can just walk down the street and buy a bagful. Slightly more ropey, admittedly, than the exalted roots of ancient China, but, used consistently over a period of several months, even an average grade ginseng will produce wonderful results. If you can obtain Heaven Grade and can afford it without fainting, take that. The results will be mega-wonderful. Otherwise go for a good tincture (East-West Herbs do a good one) or Korean ginseng. Use white ginseng for long-term treatment if possible.

Ginseng can be used by both men and women. It is a supreme tonic and rejuvenator of the whole system. It tightens tissues and enables you to function on a higher energy level. As far as sex is concerned – well, you'll sleep less. But since it gives you more energy, you probably won't mind in the least.

Schizandra

This herb is also suitable for both men and women. We have already met it in the chapter on skin rejuvenation. Schizandra has the ability to make you feel young – both inside and out. You'll both notice.

Dang Gui

In many ways perhaps the best herb for women, it makes you feel *womanly* and I like that.

THE BEST MASSAGE OIL

Is the one you like. But try this blend of three aphrodisiacs. It's really very nice. They are: benzoin, sandalwood and ginger. Together they produce an easy, relaxed hum. If you don't know what I mean (and even if you do) try it. Mix a few drops of each of the essential oils with a mild base oil such as borage or almond and apply however you like; massage, bath, perfume. Avoid sensitive areas of the body such as mouth, eyes and the genital area because these oils can sting. Other oils to try are: rose, jasmine and ylang ylang. Romantic, sensuous and beautiful.

As far as I'm concerned, you can never have too many aphrodisiacs in your life and the best of them all are histidine and Catuaba for women, Catuaba, Ashwagandha and Muira Puama for men. Try them. The effects are very nice! If you're only going to try one, make it Catuaba. Mmmmm.

PART TWO

Why Radical Rejuvenation Works

In the Foreword I said that this book is not for scientists and that's true; it is for real people who have real worries about their vitality (and the lack of it) and their degenerating bodies – people who need real solutions. But there are scientists whose investigations make you excited all over, who do not preach hopelessness nor helplessness and who are for the most part, therefore, ignored or ostracised by many of their more narrow-minded colleagues.

These adventurous minds produce *interesting* science, almost an 'alternative' science, much of which is highly relevant to the study of rejuvenation. They produce experiments which often provide the *reasons* why some approaches to rejuvenation (for instance raw foods and enzymes) work so spectacularly. In Part Two we will look at many such investigations. Apart from being interesting, reading about such studies should give you confidence in the safety and reliability of the RR approach.

In the following chapters you will meet some powerful agents of rejuvenation. Together they make up the toolkit of Radical Rejuvenation. It contains enzymes, amino acids, essential fatty acids, vitamins, minerals and herbs. In Part Two you will learn *why* this toolkit produces visible changes which are the result of improved cellular functioning.

CHAPTER FIVE

Enzymes

I'm going to start with enzymes because they are some of the most potent rejuvenating substances you can take. They will improve your looks, replacing folds of loose skin with firm, youthful outlines; increase your vitality so that you find yourself positively bouncing and grinning through your day (really!) and even help you lose unwanted fat. And when was fat ever wanted? They ease the workload on your glands, particularly the pancreas, and help your whole system work at peak efficiency. Some enzymes also protect you against free radicals. *All* enzymes (more than 2000 are known and many more are still to be discovered) play a vital role in producing the new, energetic, best 'you' that you can be. Fortunately, you don't have to take every enzyme in supplement form. Many are already in your body and many more can be made by your body. But since every enzyme is a protein, it is absolutely essential that you obtain enough *bio-available* protein from your diet. This means protein which is easily utilised by the body to produce metabolically active compounds, such as enzymes, quickly and efficiently. But guess what? The usual sources of protein in our typical, Western diet, such as meat, fish, eggs and milk are all *cooked* and what happens when you put such proteins into your body is a lot of *work*. These cooked foods are completely devoid of active enzymes because enzymes are very delicate substances and very sensitive to heat. In order to make use of the protein which these foods contain, your pancreas has to release digestive enzymes. But that places an extra load on the pancreas. With repeated consumption of cooked foods, the pancreas begins to become overworked and enlarged, showing early signs of degeneration. Many people who eat a primarily cooked diet have signs of pancreatic overload. Constant, chronic tiredness is one of those signs. So what can you do? Three things: take a high quality supplement of free form amino acids which will ensure that your body has all the necessary building blocks for the manufacture of endogenous enzymes (endogenous means 'made by the body'; 'exogenous' enzymes are the ones which come from your food or from supplements); eat a diet high in raw foods, because raw foods, quite unlike cooked foods, are a treasure trove of active, beneficial enzymes; and take biologically active enzymes directly, in the form of supplements. Here we will focus on what supplemental enzymes can do for your looks and youthfulness.

Without enzymes you would die. But it's also a lot more subtle than that; most people who live on drastically enzyme-impoverished diets are not dead – though they sometimes feel as though they are. But they know that something is missing, some level of vitality which they remember and recognise as their right continually eludes them and they don't know why. A gross lack of enzymes in the foods they eat is an enormous contributory factor in this chronic fatigue. There's no fire without enzymes. Literally, since they provide the sparks for the body's metabolic processes.

HOW TO GET SOME FIRE INTO YOUR LIFE

I like fire. I like energy and sparks. Your cells like it too. They get their sparks from enzymes. Metabolic processes which would take hours of intense heat and strong acid are over in seconds with the help of the correct enzyme. But most people aren't dynamos. Most people are tired, sluggish, overweight, limp and damp and most people are short of enzymes. Because the body relies on external supplies of certain enzymes and most people eat diets in which cooked foods predominate. Diets which are almost completely lacking in biologically active enzymes. When such chronically tired people add the correct enzymes they experience an energy they haven't known since their early teens – a time when the metabolic processes in their bodies were still running relatively smoothly. And that's not all – apart from the increased levels of energy, you will find a firmer body and smoother skin. Some enzymes will even protect you against pollution and, perhaps most important of all, if your diet contains plenty of enzymes, you will live longer. This is because you are born with an enzyme potential which will affect you throughout your lifetime. The stronger the onslaught on these enzymes, the faster you age and the shorter your life. Your body attempts to minimise this damage and synthesises enzymes as needed. This overloads your organs, particularly the pancreas. It is also not enough. Cooked foods, being completely devoid of enzymes, stress your system. Raw foods and enzyme supplements decrease the demand on your enzyme-producing systems. They will slow down the rate at which you age, prolong your life, even reverse the effects of ageing which have already taken place. You will also find that you feel brighter and happier and every one of your glands will function at its best possible level.

Here are my favourite enzyme dynamos and what they can do for you.

TOP ENZYME DYNAMOS

Lipase

Most enzymes (apart from pepsin and trypsin), by the way, end in 'ase'. The first part of their name tells you the substance on which they act, or the 'substrate'. So lipase is an enzyme which acts on, or breaks down, lipids. Fat. The next time someone tells you that you are overweight because you lack the willpower, just tell them it's because your tissue levels of lipase are depleted and you haven't yet had time to replace them. But you will. Because raw foods contain it and so do many good enzyme supplements, including Spectrumzyme. Of course, we'll be looking at many ways to help you win those firm, youthful limbs and lipase is just a beginning (in Part One you have already met many of the stars we'll be looking at in detail in Part Two – substances such as the amino acid L-carnitine and Omega 3 fatty acids). Lipase is a good beginning because a lack of this enzyme leads to a sluggish glandular system, in particular the pancreas, which has to increase its production of lipase to compensate for its lack in cooked food. Another gland severely affected by enzyme-deficient food is the thyroid. Without an efficient thyroid you cannot have a youthful, lithe body – either you will be too thin if your thyroid is out of balance and too active, or you will be overweight if your thyroid is underactive. An inadequate level of lipase in your body also leads to fat deposits in the blood vessels and can lead to hardening of the arteries. This excess of fats in the body slows the immune system right down, too. Adding supplemental lipase will help clear these fatty deposits from your body and take the strain off your glands so that efficient functioning can resume and your weight can normalise. Your arteries and immune system will be smiling, too.

Amylase

This enzyme is responsible for the digestion of carbohydrates. It can also, together with lipase, clear the lungs of mucus and destroy viruses, such as herpes. In one study it was found that patients with psoriasis, dermatitis and pruritis had low levels of amylase in their blood. Another study showed lowered levels of amylase in patients suffering from liver diseases such as cirrhosis, hepatitis and cholecystitis (inflammation of the gall bladder). Restoring these patients' amylase levels brought an improvement in their liver condition. Most people over the age of thirty-five or so are deficient in amylase if they have been habitually consuming cooked food because their tissue levels of this enzyme – and other enzymes, too – have been depleted by such a diet. Young people have been shown to release much greater quantities of amylase, for instance, in response to a meal high in carbohydrates than older people. People deficient in this enzyme will experience problems with carbohydrate foods. Problems such as bloating, constipation, flatulence. Even in themselves, of course, these conditions lead to lowered vitality and youthfulness. But they lead to further degeneration if the underlying cause, the lack of enzyme activity, is not corrected. This sort of degeneration, as we have seen, may manifest in the liver, on the skin or in the joints in the form of arthritis.

When you supplement your diet with adequate levels of amylase, not only will you be avoiding degeneration of your body, you will also find the beginnings of freedom from cravings for starchy, nutrient-deficient foods such as bread and cakes. Amylase is your friend. Add it to your RR programme and let yourself shine!

Proteolytic Enzymes

In many ways these are the real stars of enzyme therapy. Proteolytic enzymes break down protein. An excess of protein, particularly of animal origin, has been linked to a myriad of degenerative conditions resulting in the visible changes which we call ageing and in a shortened life span. A diet which is high in protein results in an increased rate of amyloids deposited in connective tissues and organs. Amyloids are toxic compounds which are the result of protein metabolism. They are deposited in the cells themselves and cause great degeneration there. A diet high in protein also causes an imbalance between calcium and magnesium in the body, causing all sorts of skeletal and tooth problems which can result in osteoporosis and weakened teeth. Meat has been shown to cause a loss of calcium from the body. Meat also leads to the formation of high levels of ammonia, a substance which is highly toxic to your cells.

A very interesting hypothesis concerning the role of excess protein in ageing was put forward by a family of three German physicians, all with the surname Wendt. With the aid of electron microscopy they were able to show that excess protein clogs the basement membrane, which is a filter between small blood vessels (capillaries) and cells. When this filter is clean and clear, nutrients and oxygen pass through quickly and efficiently from the blood into the cell, where they are needed. Similarly, waste products of cell metabolism pass out of the cell quickly and do not poison the interior of the cell. However, the more protein your diet contains, especially protein of animal origin, the less efficient this process becomes, due to the clogging of the filter, the basement membrane. This, of course, is the beginning of degeneration, of sluggish cell functioning and auto-toxification of cells. If this process continues for long enough the clogging becomes so bad that insoluble protein begins to line the capillary and arterial walls, leading to arteriosclerosis, high blood pressure and adult diabetes. Of course, your cells aren't getting the nutrients and oxygen they need. Any wonder that you feel tired? *But* when you avoid all protein of animal origin, add lots of protein-digesting (proteolytic) enzymes to your diet and eat all your food in its uncooked, raw state (raw protein is easily assimilated and does not lead to this clogging of the basement membrane), nutrients and oxygen can go straight through into the cells. No problem. Your basement membrane becomes as thin and porous and efficient as that of a baby and that can't be bad.

And before you rush out and buy up all the supplies of proteolytic enzymes in your neighbourhood, let me give you a few more reasons why you should. In fact, it is one BIG reason – your pancreas.

The pancreas is the first of your organs to be hit by both the chemicals in the food you eat and its low enzyme content. As you have already seen in the section on lipase, in the absence of sufficient enzymes necessary for the digestion of food, your pancreas takes the load; it simply must manufacture these enzymes itself, if they are not present in your food. It becomes overworked. Here, yet again, we see a link between some common degenerative diseases and an enzyme-deficient way of eating – diabetes. A person with an overworked pancreas begins to show some of the early signs of this illness. Lesser symptoms include, as we have already seen with amylase, what is commonly known as a 'food allergy'. Since these important proteolytic enzymes are involved in the regulation of inflammation, low levels will lead to an excessive inflammatory response. There are two kinds: a kinin- and a histamine-mediated inflammatory response. Proteolytic enzymes control them both. When such a response follows the ingestion of food, we call it 'food allergy'. Proteolytic enzymes, together with lipase and amylase, taken at the beginning of every meal for at least three months, have greatly helped people suffering from such allergies.

Insufficient levels of proteolytic enzymes also result in low levels of amino acids, since your body can only make incomplete use of the protein you ingest and the increase in inflammatory reactions described above is the start of a chain of reactions which eventually lead to cell degeneration, even cancer. The low levels of amino acids which come from low levels of these enzymes result in deficiencies of hormones (including the hormone from the thyroid which is necessary for the maintenance of a slim body), tissues, other enzymes (thus increasing deficiencies of enzymes throughout the body in a cascading reaction) and antibodies, making you particularly susceptible to infections. Deficiencies of B6 and zinc can also be a consequence of inadequate amino acid levels. All because of low levels of proteolytic enzymes.

You can buy them in supplemental form; here are some names to look out for:

protease
bromelain
papain

Now all you have to do is go out and get some! Oh, and I don't recommend pancreatic extract or any other animal-derived enzyme products. There are plenty of plant-derived enzyme products around. One of the best is Spectrumzyme made by BioCare.

So far we have looked at enzymes which are involved in the digestion of food. The typical results of supplementing your diet with these factors are an increase in energy, emotional balance and a light and more youthful body. There is another group of enzymes sold in supplemental form on the market. They are not directly involved in the digestion of food, but they provide you with youth and good looks all the same. They protect you against damage caused by pollution and metabolic inefficiency, as well as damage caused by rancid oils, which are very common in our diet as a result of frying, long storage, overprocessing and the simple but inevitable action of air every time you open your bottle of high-quality, cold-pressed walnut, hazelnut or linseed oil. (The addition of vitamins E and C, as mentioned in Chapter One, is one safety measure designed to minimise rancidity as a result of exposure to air.) Until recently many scientists, with superior arrogance, regarded supplementation with these anti-oxidant enzymes as a waste of time and money. No more. Even taken orally, some of these enzymes have been shown to exert highly beneficial protection against free radical damage. The one sort of 'radical' that you definitely don't want!

You will find more pollution fighters in the chapters on amino acids, herbs, vitamins and minerals. Here we'll make friends with some rather lively enzymes.

SOD

Let's start with the liveliest one. Not only is it a very active enzyme in the body, it has given rise to much heated debate over its usefulness when supplemented by oral administration. Its full name is superoxide dismutase and its role is to protect the body against too much oxygen. Because too much oxygen can be as harmful as too little and an agent which protects you against the effects of too much oxygen also protects you against cancer and the deterioration associated with ageing. Opinion is (hotly) divided on the value of SOD tablets taken by mouth, although *injections* of this enzyme have been proved to be highly beneficial as an anti-ageing substance. The argument put forward by the critics of the oral administration of SOD are the same as those against the use of enzyme supplements in general – that these enzymes are digested in the gut as any other protein would be and cannot, therefore, survive to exert any therapeutic action in the body. This has already been proved not to be the case – many orally administered enzymes do survive digestion intact and make effective therapeutic agents. A more serious argument against the oral use of SOD is that it is too large to pass into the bloodstream. As we shall see, some beneficial supplements do exist which actually have the effect of increasing the levels of SOD in your body.

SOD is one of the more delicate enzymes and enzymes are delicate. What happens when you take SOD by mouth is that it gets destroyed in the acidic environment in the stomach. This applies especially to bovine-derived material which means most of the SOD tablets in your health food shop. However, SOD derived from plants manages to survive just long enough to make contact with the receptors in the stomach wall and increase your own output of this enzyme, as well as the two other anti-oxidant enzymes, glutathione peroxidase and catalase. To obtain this highly desirable effect (oxidation is a BIG factor in ageing. You don't want it. Anti-oxidants stop oxidation. See section on Free Radicals at the end of this chapter) you need to take an effective product and you need to take it on an empty stomach to maximise receptor interaction. BioCare's OxyPlex fits the bill perfectly. Instead of taking OxyPlex, however, you could simply eat lots of sprouted seeds, pulses and grains, especially wheat sprouts. These are all loaded with beneficial enzymes, known *and* those still to be discovered! Sprouts are very cheap, too. For details on sprouting consult Chapter Ten 'Diet and Lifestyle'.

Whether you wish to try SOD itself or not, make sure that you take supplements of selenium and zinc, which will ensure that your body is able to manufacture adequate levels of SOD and another anti-oxidant enzyme, glutathione peroxidase. There is a form of SOD which contains copper. Although, as I have said earlier, normally copper supplementation is unnecessary, excessive intakes of vitamin C, zinc, calcium, raw meat or toxic metals such as mercury and lead and high levels of sulphide and molybdenum can all produce copper deficiencies. Do not exceed daily supplements of zinc over 30 mg without professional guidance. Do not, however, take supplements of copper unless you know you have a definite deficiency of this mineral.

Catalase

SOD gets rid of dangerous, activated superoxide oxygen molecules, forming hydrogen peroxide in the process. Two enzymes inactivate this hydrogen peroxide: glutathione peroxidase and catalase. You can take both glutathione (glutathione is an amino acid which stimulates glutathione peroxidase activity) and catalase orally with excellent results and no controversy, for once. Taken orally, both have been shown to be highly active. Instead of hydrogen peroxide, you're left with water and a de-activated oxygen. Oh, and a healthier, more youthful body!

WHY FREE RADICALS MAKE YOU OLD

Free radicals are highly unstable, extremely reactive molecules. They have an unpaired, free electron in their outer orbit which gives them a positive charge. In order to balance this charge (all molecules prefer to be in a balanced, neutral state) these free radicals become trouble makers and 'steal' electrons from other molecules in a process which the originator of the Free Radical hypothesis, Dr Denham Harman, likened to internal radiation. Depending on which molecules the free radicals encounter and attack, a variety of degenerative changes will occur. Over time, these changes produce what we call 'ageing'. For example, say that free radicals from a smoke-filled room enter your bloodstream, when these molecules make contact with the molecules of your blood capillaries, they will start a cascade of electron 'borrowing'; in their effort to balance their own charge, free radicals cause the formation of many more unstable, charged molecules and your capillaries will begin to experience damage which will, with time, become extensive, causing cardiovascular problems, restricting circulation and greatly decreasing the amount of oxygen and nutrients delivered to your cells. If, on the other hand, the free radicals encounter the collagen molecules which provide strength and support for your skin, they break the bonds between collagen molecules. The result is weakened skin structure – wrinkles.

Depending on the tissues which these highly active molecules attack, similar tissue damage and cell destruction can produce symptoms and conditions such as arthritis, cataracts, cancer, age spots, heart disease and arteriosclerosis.

Free radicals are a normal by-product of metabolism and, as we have just seen, our bodies are equipped to deal with them. The problem is that suddenly, due to our modern lifestyle, our bodies are daily encountering concentrations of free radicals far exceeding the amounts that they are equipped to handle. Sunlight, smoke, stress and air pollution are all concentrated sources of free radicals. So are: cooking, especially when it results in browned foods such as charcoal-grilled meat, toast or roasted nuts. Heated oils are one of the most potent sources of free radicals. Even oils exposed to sunlight and air produce these harmful compounds. So the in-built free radical deactivators such as SOD, glutathione peroxidase and catalase need a big helping hand. Which is what supplementation is all about. Fortunately, there are many effective ways to minimise free radical damage in your body. These include the use of amino acids, vitamins, minerals and certain herbs as well as some raw foods, many of which have potent anti-oxidant properties. You will find them all discussed in detail in the following chapters. The good news is that all these beneficial factors will provide assistance against ageing, whatever the cause. We have already seen that excessive protein consumption, liver malfunction, cooked foods and pancreatic overload also cause degenerative changes. The measures in the RR programme will help to protect you against these, and other causes of ageing, too.

CHAPTER SIX

Amino Acids

I once read in a magazine that what you need in California is a thin arse and fat hair. It's all too easy to get it the wrong way round. Amino acids are for all of us who are Californian at heart but who keep getting those fat and thin bits muddled up.

.As we saw in the previous chapter, too much protein is detrimental to health and youthfulness. Amino acids taken as supplements to an all-raw (or a high-raw) diet are a different thing altogether. Because these amino acids, if they are what is known as 'free form', are absorbed and utilised by the body without needing to be broken down. They do not cause the dangerous effects of improperly digested cooked protein. What they *can* do, however, will astonish you. Much of the research on amino acids has been pioneered by Dr Robert Erdmann.

AMINOS AGAINST AGEING

Recently scientists tested a substance on old people. Given by injection, this substance produced marked effects on the appearance of the test subjects – their skin became clearer, more pliable and wrinkles were less visible, their cholesterol levels normalised, joints moved more freely and easily, they had more stamina and resistance to disease. Interested? Unfortunately, it had some unpleasant side-effects and the tests were discontinued. However, if you'd like to, you can experience the effects of this substance for yourself. Without injections and without side effects. The substance in question was the human growth hormone and because it was injected and because it was in a synthetic form, it produced effects which were not entirely beneficial. But there is an alternative to injected, synthetic growth hormone: amino acid supplements. Certain amino acids will help your body *make* more of its own, natural growth hormone. The two amino acids which can be used to increase your own production of this anti-ageing hormone are arginine and lysine. Some researchers have also found glycine to be effective. When you use these aminos you will find that your muscles actually increase in firmness, seem more defined and you look leaner all over. Not skinny and not masculine (though men who take them look more masculine – it's all due to the fact that nutritional factors work with the body. Unlike drugs, they do not produce strong, undesirable and unnatural effects). The effects you do get are strong, glowing and alive.

If you suffer from herpes, choose ornithine instead of arginine. Lysine is fine to use – in fact, it has been found to be highly beneficial by decreasing the severity and frequency of herpes attacks.

Always take all amino supplements with lots of water. Growth hormone stimulators should be taken last thing at night with a good B complex. Start with 1500 mg (that's one and a half grams) of your chosen amino supplement. Some people take more but higher doses should be monitored by an expert experienced in the use of amino acids. If you are lactating, expecting a baby or there may be a chance of conception, do not take these growth hormone stimulators.

There are other ways of increasing your growth hormone levels. One of them is exercise. Due to the release of this hormone, your metabolic rate remains high for some time following a good session of aerobic exercise. It doesn't take too long – fifteen minutes a day is sufficient to get those hormones flowing. And have you noticed how your skin glows and your body and face look so much younger when you start an exercise programme? Increased growth hormone production as well as improved circulation are responsible for these welcome changes.

Children produce very high levels of growth hormone. The levels of production are highest at night, during deep sleep. I have noticed that people who change over to a completely raw diet begin to experience very deep sleep again, just like they used to during childhood. So it's possible that more growth hormone is produced on raw food diets. If so, that would be another possible explanation for the anti-ageing effects of eating your food uncooked. And that's on top of the enzymes, vitamins, minerals and other vitality factors found in raw foods!

Fasting and undereating also increase your levels of growth hormone. In fact, consistent undereating has been found to be a very effective way of increasing life span. This does not mean living on diet foods, which are highly depleted, denatured foods; undereating is the art of eating less while keeping the level of youth-enhancing nutrients in your diet extremely high. As far as I'm concerned, undereating should always depend exclusively on a superb, raw food diet which includes a liberal dose of the tonics and supplements recommended in this book. For beauty and youthfulness I recommend as much of the high-enzyme raw foods as you wish to eat. You won't overeat. Drastic cuts in food intake have not impressed me as an effective method of attaining a juicy, young body. Quite the opposite. I have seen many people become quite dried out and old looking because they tried to subsist on a very extreme diet. The Radical Rejuvenation Diet is not extreme; it isn't 'normal', but it isn't extreme. And just as well that it is not normal – look where 'normal' is leading you!

LOOKING AFTER YOUR PANCREAS

Here's that gland again – responsible for the manufacture of insulin and many important enzymes. The health of this organ is incredibly important to both youthfulness and longevity. We've already seen how supplements of digestive enzymes can help to keep your pancreas young and unstressed. You can help it even more if you make sure that you take a full complement of free form amino acids every day. This is important because these easily utilised protein building blocks assist the pancreas in manufacturing all the enzymes you need – enzymes are made of protein. And a diet full of *cooked* protein is actually pretty poor in *utilisable* amino acids. Many are denatured by the cooking process, still more are coagulated and difficult to digest, which places a double load on your poor old pancreas, because it has to produce greater concentrations of digestive enzymes to break down proteins too poor to replenish the amino acids used in the process. But with a raw food diet, supplemental enzymes and a full complement of amino acids, your pancreas can begin to recover. As it does, you will notice you are far less irritable as your sugar levels begin to stabilise. Also, since the pancreas is involved in your whole hormone system as well as closely linked with the functioning of your liver and adrenal glands, the effect of restored functioning will benefit all of you. Stress will be less of a problem. And stress does make your hair go grey – you lose an awful lot of B vitamins when you are under stress and low levels of these wonderful vitamins are related to greying hair.

Making certain that you receive your full quota of amino acids every day has other benefits which show in the way you look. Your face and body will be visibly firmer when you take aminos regularly. I hope you have noticed that I am not talking about *protein* here but amino acids. They are not one and the same when it comes to the efficiency and youthfulness of your body. Amino acids are what your body needs. Protein is what your body usually gets and has to make the best of. And this is, as we have seen, not always as easy as it ought to be. *Plus* amino acids contain no fat. Getting the picture? If you want firm, juicy and sexy, get some aminos.

CARNITINE

The Wild One – this amino acid is amazing. I love it. The best Christmas/birthday present you can give yourself is a course of carnitine. L-carnitine is what you need to take. Put very simply, carnitine breaks down fat both in the arteries and in the muscles, giving you a firmer outline and a healthier heart all in one go. It gives you incredible energy, greater stamina and makes you feel sexy. It even protects you against ketosis should you ever wish to try that low calorie diet again (which I hope you won't – raw foods are what you're aiming for not calorie restriction).

Carnitine works by making more fuel (fat, to you and me, in the form of fatty acids) available to the mitochondria, which are organelles in the cell responsible for the generation of ENERGY. The faster these are supplied with fatty acids, the higher your energy. So now you know what to do when you are feeling pale and wan. Take some carnitine and get those fatty acids out of your arteries and 'love handles' and into your smile and stride! You'll soon be racing around so fast no one will be able to keep up with you (unless they're on carnitine too!).

GLUTATHIONE

We have already seen how dangerous free radicals from pollution, the sun and rancid fats can cause harmful chain reactions in the body which can lead to a loss of integrity of the body tissues. When this happens in the skin it's called wrinkles and we call the process 'ageing'. But you know now that what you are looking at is a faulty biochemistry that can be fixed. Like SOD, the powerful oxidation fighter glutathione peroxidase that we met in the enzyme chapter doesn't survive the digestion process very well, so if it's taken as an oral supplement its usefulness is slight. However, you can take these enzymes in from sprouts such as sprouted wheat and in this way your own production of these valuable enzymes is increased.

Another way to increase your levels of glutathione peroxidase is by taking a supplement of the amino acid glutathione. It helps increase levels of the pollution fighter glutathione synthetase as well as having anti-oxidant properties – overall it carries quite a punch.

However, glutathione itself is also vulnerable to the digestive process. It's often more effective to take the three amino acids which together make up glutathione; this will give you all of the benefits mentioned above. These three amino acids are cysteine, glutamic acid and glycine.

Glutathione is especially helpful in protecting your skin against sun damage and airborne pollution. It has also been used to calm down hyperactive children (use glutathione itself for this purpose rather than the three-amino mix). It will protect you against lead and mercury toxicity too, and any other heavy metals will also be safely disposed of.

METHIONINE AND CYSTEINE

These two amino acids have a very strong affinity for skin; cysteine has a particularly strong relationship with hair as well. I have found that organic sulphur is even better than cysteine in producing thick hair but this may be due to the excellent quality of the sulphur supplement. Both methionine and cysteine contain sulphur and so at least a part of their activity will be due to this element.

As an internal (my favourite method for producing real, visible and lasting changes in the way you look) anti-ageing skin treatment, cysteine is hard to beat. Twenty-five per cent of your skin protein is actually cysteine. This amino acid provides the structural strength of the collagen fibres, keeping your skin taut, smooth, elastic and wrinkle-free. As we've seen, free radicals attach themselves to the molecules in this skin structure and begin to disrupt its integrity. But if you take lots of cysteine (as well as other anti-oxidants) on a daily basis you will prevent the destruction that normally accompanies an attack by free radicals. They will bond with the cysteine and leave your skin alone.

Methionine, while lacking cysteine's affinity for the skin and hair, still provides a remarkably effective protective action against the damaging effects of pollution and the sun.

GLYCINE

I have a soft spot for this one. Maybe it's because it decreases sugar cravings or because it increases growth hormone release. Mostly, though, I think it's because it makes the skin so elastic. If you have any stretch marks, try glycine (and zinc – more on zinc when we get to vitamins and minerals). Your skin contains even more glycine than it does cysteine. Too little glycine makes collagen brittle and this brittleness produces stretch marks. The good news is that with glycine your skin can maintain and even regain flexibility and suppleness. The brittleness will be eliminated and in its place will be the sort of skin that moves and flexes like much younger skin.

Adding vitamin C to the above mentioned nutrients (cysteine, glycine and zinc) will strengthen your collagen greatly. This means supple, smooth and wrinkle-free flesh. Mmmmm.

RR IN ACTION

A young dog started having grand mal epileptic seizures. She would fall to the ground, jerking her limbs and foaming at the mouth. If she tried to stand up she would fall down again even after the worst of the fit had passed. She would remain very dazed and weak for hours afterwards. She was given magnesium taurate (which has been found to be helpful in human epilepsy) and calcium, together with valerian, skullcap, passion flower and Gotu Kola tinctures. Her seizures stopped as soon as the treatment commenced and re-appeared whenever there was a lapse in the treatment. However, after just four months of treatment the herbs and supplements were stopped and the seizures did not reappear. Now she has a maintenance dose of herbs every now and then and is a very alert and lively dog. This case illustrates that this sort of treatment approach is certainly not 'just in the mind' since the owners forgot to inform the dog what the supplements and tinctures were for! Also, it shows clearly one of the greatest wonders of all – that herbs and supplements, when correctly employed, are capable of curing. That is, the problem goes away for good and does not need constant medication.

CHAPTER SEVEN

Essential Fatty Acids

Nowadays fats are trendy. There are Bad Fats (from meat, cheese and milk) and Good Fats (from vegetable sources). Good Fats are in and Bad Fats are out. Except it is a little more complicated than that. At least for me. Because I have found a few things about the Good Guys which aren't so good. So the bad news first.

There is (almost) no such thing as a cold-pressed oil. The friction during extraction produces HEAT. Not trivial, friendly warmth, but real heat, which cooks and destroys the oil and produces free radicals. In Chapter One I suggested the use of walnut, hazelnut and linseed oil on salads and I still think they play a valuable role in what I call the Transition Time – that period when you are becoming familiar with RR or cheating – but it is very difficult indeed to make sure that the oil you're using is not going to produce havoc in your body. The very process of expressing it, together with light (most oils are sold in transparent bottles), age (the longer the oil remains in contact with air, the more damaging the free radicals that are formed) and warmth (how many shops keep their cold-pressed oils in the fridge?) – all this amounts to a potential health disaster. I first became aware that something was wrong with the 'right' and 'good' oils when I developed a very stiff back while eating a very healthy diet. I was only in my early thirties, yet whenever I bent down I could scarcely straighten up again! It worried and puzzled me in equal measure for a while until I removed olive oil from my diet. Extra virgin organic it was, so I thought I couldn't get a better product. When I stopped using it my back returned to normal within one week. Some time later, when I began using olive oil again, I developed a very painful cracking jaw. It hurt so much and was deteriorating so rapidly that I began to worry whether soon I would be able to chew at all. My dentist informed me it was a very common problem (even he had it, he said) and made an appointment to install a plate. It didn't sound jolly and nice, this plate business. It sounded OLD. I stopped the olive oil and cancelled the appointment. My jaw stopped hurting within two days and the pain has not returned.

Another time I was using walnut oil which, at first, helped my husband's painful and damaged knee joints and helped several children with bed-wetting problems. But after a while the joints became painful again and some of my clients, as well as my daughter and I, began to develop dry patches on the backs of our hands, a condition normally associated with an excess of saturated fat from animal sources. But this time it seemed to be linked with the use of walnut oil which is high in Omega 3 fatty acids.

At that point I decided to do some thinking. It went like this:

1. Essential fatty acids are essential to human health and have a particular affinity for the joints and skin.
2. Oils which contain these fatty acids are extremely fragile and vulnerable to free radical formation.

3. Modern technology, for the most part, does not take point 2 into account.
4. Oils, even in health food shops, are sold in transparent bottles and kept unrefrigerated. Light, both natural and artificial, and warmth are important factors in producing rancidity and free radical formation in oils.

So rancidity of the oil is one explanation for the stiff joints and flaky skin. This is a good explanation if your symptoms appear soon after taking the recommended four to five tablespoons of walnut oil or three tablespoons of linseed oil. If, however, your symptoms appear some time after you begin supplementation or if you are taking larger than recommended doses of Omega 3 oils, consider the possibility that you are getting too much of a good thing. This is possible with many supplements, for example with the fat-soluble vitamins A and D and, to a lesser extent, with E. So if you have experienced a flare-up of existing symptoms cut down the dose of oil or vitamin you are using. The symptoms should then disappear within days.

Returning to the issue of the olive oil, it may not have been rancidity that was the cause in this case. This oil, being monounsaturated, is not very easily oxidised. But it was precisely this factor which made olive oil a health hazard for me; it contains almost no polyunsaturated EFAs, so when it is used as the source of fat in the diet, the results are similar to the situation which occurs with a predominance of saturated fats. The availability of EFAs is compromised; saturated and monounsaturated fats interfere in the metabolic pathways of EFAs. Some other fats of plant origin which are not suitable for healthy diets are palm oil and coconut oil. They are both high in saturated fat.

Now for the good news. I am still a real oil freak – just a careful oil freak. The most helpful advice I can give you is to buy the best oils you can find. If it doesn't say organic and unrefined, it isn't.

This is the checklist for the best oils:

- Sold in opaque bottles or at least kept out of direct light.

- 'Unrefined' and 'organic' are the key words to look for.
- Gravity settled, not filtered.
- Kept under refrigeration in the shop and at home.
- Taste good. This is quite a good indicator of quality. Unrefined oils taste sweet. Even linseed. Though this one may not be your favourite taste, it should still taste sweet rather than bitter.

You will probably find it difficult to find a product which meets all these criteria, but this list should provide you with a useful method of assessing the quality of oils. Some oils certainly meet most of the above criteria but can be on the expensive side, so it's fine to go for a cheaper but good walnut oil and see how it suits you.

For added protection against free radical formation, add 400 i.u. of vitamin E and about half a teaspoon of vitamin C powder or thirty drops of ascorbyl glycerate (VitaSorb C) to each 250 ml of your oil *as soon* as you have opened the bottle. It is also a good idea to take a good multi-vitamin and mineral preparation which will supply you with selenium, chromium, zinc, vitamin C and vitamin E. Consider taking extra doses of vitamin C (so that you are taking 500 mg each day), vitamin E (100 mg a day at least and anything up to 400 mg per day which is a safe and beneficial level but one that needs to be worked up to) and beta carotene (1500–7500 i.u. daily).

Another possible way of getting EFAs into your life is to eat the nuts and seeds which contain them. And this, also, can be complicated. Because cooking methods such as grilling and frying destroy the fatty acids, forming those same nasty free radicals. Baking is also harmful and even eating the raw seeds and nuts can have their difficulties. This is because nuts and seeds (and grains and pulses) contain enzyme inhibitors to prevent them from sprouting under unfavourable conditions. But you know by now that enzymes are good for you so you don't want them inhibited! No worries. You deactivate the inhibitors by simply soaking the seeds, nuts, grains and pulses before you eat them. Complete deactivation of enzyme inhibitors takes twenty-four hours. You can speed up the process by adding rejuvelac or enzyme powder to the soaking water and stirring well. That way you can eat hazelnuts, almonds, cashews, brazil nuts, pecans and walnuts after eight hours. If you feel heavy after eating nuts, the enzyme inhibitors have not been fully deactivated. Some seeds, such as sunflower, and pulses, such as mung bean sprouts, sprout after less than twenty-four hours and are therefore safe to eat at an earlier stage. In fact, sunflower seeds are best eaten before then, otherwise they begin to lose their vitality unless kept covered with water or refrigerated.

You can also obtain a very high quality product called Nutri-Flax made from linseed which has been carefully heated to retain the beneficial enzymes but to deactivate the enzyme inhibitors, although I am a little wary of heat processing where fats are concerned. Nutri-Flax contains added vitamin B6 and zinc. Linseed contains a B6 inhibitor and zinc is an essential mineral factor in the metabolism of fatty acids. This product may be poured on to your salad, included in drinks, mixes and smoothies.

Given the difficulties of obtaining active, healthy sources of EFAs, why should we bother? Well, just take a look at the conditions where the use of EFAs have been beneficial:

cancer
alcoholism
obesity
schizophrenia
allergies
asthma
eczema
arthritis
drug addiction
depression
fatigue
heart disease

Impressive, eh? EFAs play an important role in the functioning of your immune system. My own observations have led me to the conclusion that varicose veins are also linked with a deficiency and imbalance of EFAs. Beginning to see why these oils are so important, especially to Westerners? One more thing before we take a closer look at the importance of fatty acids to rejuvenation. We've seen that amino acids, taken as a complete spectrum supplement, are powerful but taking the two together, EFAs and aminos, is close to miraculous! The idea of mixing the two is based on the work of Dr Joanna Budwig (following in the footsteps of Professor Meyerhoff) who found that mixing a protein with EFAs produces fantastic results, including the disappearance of cancerous tumours, increased skin elasticity and an enhanced sense of well-being and energy. Apparently the Cherokee Indians used a similar combination of protein and linseed to build strength, muscle and stamina in their warriors. I have modified it by using a blend of free form amino acids as the source of protein with excellent results. The reason for this modification is my conviction, based on close observation, experience and evidence, that animal proteins contribute greatly to body degeneration. Also, free form aminos provide the most effective and the most easily assimilated protein source there is. Try it. This combination gives you a real energy boost, repairs skin cells, joints, internal organs including the heart and even gives you shiny hair! The most effective amino acids are the ones containing sulphur – we have already met cysteine and methionine. Taurine is another one.

So good luck with the EFAs. Think of the benefits and remember the cautions. The only price for being careful with this one is being younger and fitter and less likely to fall victim to disease. So go for it. Rather a good price to pay I'd say.

TYPES OF FATTY ACIDS

Here are some technical facts about fatty acids.

Polyunsaturated Fatty Acids

These are fats with many (poly) free (unsaturated) carbon atoms in their molecular structure, forming what are known as double bonds. This sort of arrangement makes polyunsaturated fatty acids unstable and reactive; both beneficial and potentially dangerous. This is because by virtue of their instability and flexibility they are prone to oxidation and the production of dangerous free radicals. Polyunsaturated fatty acids have a 'healthy' image but in reality they can only be beneficial if they are not oxidised. Oxidation of polyunsaturated fatty acids occurs rapidly under the following conditions: heat, ranging from long-term exposure to innocuous room temperatures up to the high temperatures reached during frying, especially deep frying, but including the gentler stir frying and sautéing, as well as the severe, extreme temperatures employed during the manufacture of margarine and some refined vegetable oils. Oxidation also occurs with the action of light on these polyunsaturated fatty acids, both natural and artificial. This means that most oils, including so-called 'cold-pressed' oils, have been damaged to some extent and contain free radicals in varying amounts. This also applies to the fatty acids found in whole seeds and nuts although to a somewhat lesser extent. The best thing to do is to use seeds and nuts, soak them whenever you can prior to use and use oils sparingly, always keeping them refrigerated and away from light. A high intake of polyunsaturated fatty acids increases your requirement for vitamin E.

Essential Fatty Acids

These are polyunsaturated fatty acids which cannot be manufactured by the body and are essential for health. A daily intake of these EFAs is therefore necessary. The best sources of EFAs are linseeds, also called flax seeds (or linseed oil), walnuts (or walnut oil), hazelnuts (or hazelnut oil) and fatty fish such as salmon, mackerel, sardines and herring or cod liver oil. Remember the precautions already mentioned when considering the use of oils; you will probably find that used sparingly in salad dressings they are acceptable. I do not recommend the use of fish and fish liver oils as EFA sources, but if you choose to use animal products then you may wish to choose this type of fish as part of your diet. Children have very high requirements for essential fatty acids.

OMEGA 3 AND OMEGA 6 FATTY ACIDS

Both of these are essential fatty acids. Significantly, their occurrence in the human diet has fallen to 20 per cent or less of the amount obtained from food a hundred years ago. Omega 3 fatty acids are more unsaturated than Omega 6. An Omega 3 EFA is one in which unsaturation (the first double bond between carbon atoms) begins three carbons from the end (omega) carbon. In Omega 6 EFAs the first double bond occurs six carbons from the end. Linseed is a superb source of both the relatively scarce Omega 3 EFAs and the Omega 6 EFAs. Walnuts and hazelnuts also contain both kinds of EFAs, but in less favourable proportions. Sunflower seeds contain predominantly Omega 6 EFAs, while almonds are rich in Omega 9 oils which are not considered essential.

Omega 3 and Omega 6 fatty acids are essential for the normal growth and brain development of children, the prevention of dry, flaky skin and in the treatment of eczema and psoriasis. They have many metabolic roles. Omega 3 and Omega 6 EFAs are prostaglandin precursors and thus play a role in regulating inflammation and are involved in many bodily processes involving hormones and in mediating immunity, the integrity of cell membranes, maintenance of cholesterol metabolism, motor coordination, muscle strength, circulatory disorders and rheumatic and arthritic disease.

EVENING PRIMROSE OIL

Together with borage and blackcurrant seed oils, evening primrose oil is a rich source of gamma linolenic acid (GLA). This fatty acid is very important in the Omega 6 metabolic pathway. Some people have difficulty manufacturing GLA and an external source in the form of a supplement is often very helpful in certain cases of eczema, psoriasis and multiple sclerosis.

Cis- and Trans- Fatty Acids

These are dangerous fatty acids produced by the oxygenation of fatty acids of all sorts during processing with heat or after exposure to light. These fatty acids wreak havoc in the human body and greatly contribute to ageing. Polyunsaturated fatty acids (including Omega 3 and Omega 6 EFAs) are the most vulnerable but the fatty acids in animal fats and butter (for example stearic and butyric fatty acids) are also susceptible. Among their many detrimental effects, these harmful fatty acids increase low-density lipoproteins or LDL (bad) cholesterol and decrease high-density lipoproteins or HDL (good) cholesterol and greatly damage the heart and the whole circulatory system.

Margarine

Once sold as a healthful food, it is nothing of the sort. It is known as 'plasticised oil' in the industry and that is a pretty accurate name for it. Hydrogenation is the technical term for the process which changes liquid oils to a solid, spreadable mass. During hydrogenation a hydrogen atom is added to the free carbon atoms in a polyunsaturated fatty acid, making the oil saturated and solid at room temperature. This process is probably the most dangerous process that oils can be subjected to. Hydrogenated margarines can be extremely damaging to the human body, producing vast amounts of free radicals. The recently introduced non-hydrogenated margarines are not much better since the oil used as the starting point is probably still subjected to high temperatures and light during its manufacture.

Butter

The saturated fats in butter interfere with EFA metabolic pathways and so can create deficits *even if* your intake of the essential fatty acids is adequate. However, small amounts of butter are preferable to any amount of margarine! If you can obtain raw, unsalted butter, that's even better. Or try using mashed avocado as a spread or make your own fresh, raw nut butters.

About Fat-free Diets

In a word, don't even think about it! Unless you yearn for wrinkles and dry skin, awful hair, irritability and flabby muscles! Just make sure you're eating the right sort of fat – essential fatty acids.

RR IN ACTION

A boy of seven had suffered from bed-wetting for two years. It bothered him but outwardly he seemed fine about it. It wasn't until the condition cleared that his mother realised how much happier he suddenly was. His treatment was simple: two dessertspoons of walnut oil every morning. When the little boy discovered that the oil helped him stay dry in the night, he made sure his mum didn't forget his daily dose! The amount of oil was gradually decreased until it was no longer necessary. Often a teaspoon of the oil or some linseed or walnuts every day will stop the problem from recurring.

CHAPTER EIGHT

Vitamins and Minerals

Vitamins were my first love. Years ago I remember reading Gayerlord Hauser and Lelord Kordell and finding out that a lack of riboflavin led to bloodshot eyes and later eating dried milk powder from the tin. It didn't work. My eyes stayed red. Somehow it didn't matter; I have since read every book on nutrition and supplements that I could afford and many that I couldn't. And I have found out that there are many vitamins that really *do* affect the way you look, some even capable of repairing sun-damaged skin (with perseverance) and greatly increasing the pliability and smoothness of your complexion. Riboflavin can, by the way, diminish those unsightly red blood vessels in your eyes, but dried milk isn't the best place to look for it.

In this chapter you will not find a boring list of vitamins and their general function in the body. This chapter will show you the real stars – those vitamins that play a key role in looking young.

VITAMINS

Vitamins are either water or fat soluble. The water-soluble ones are the B complex, vitamin C and the bioflavonoids and are measured in milligrams. The fat-soluble vitamins are A, D, E and K and are measured in International Units, or i.u. for short. Beta carotene, which is also water soluble, is often measured in i.u. as well as milligrams.

Vitamins are vital to enzyme function, which explains some of their essential actions in looking good. An enzyme consists of a protein and a co-enzyme This co-enzyme is often a vitamin, usually from the B complex group. So a deficiency of vitamins is another good way of depriving your body of optimum enzyme function and forcing your cells to limp along to gradual decline and death instead of sparking on all cylinders and providing you with youthful allure.

Let's begin by looking at the rejuvenation vitamins.

Vitamin C and Bioflavonoids

Vitamin C is famous and rightly so. For a start, you have to get it from your food, as your body is unable to manufacture this vitamin. But did you know that some oranges in supermarkets have been found to contain no vitamin C whatsoever? Even the freshest fruit has antioxidant powers and vitamin C levels way below those available from supplements. Make fruit a huge part of your rejuvenation diet, certainly, but consider vitamin C supplements a necessity *especially* if you live in a polluted area, if you smoke, drink alcohol or coffee, eat fried or animal food, or if you work very hard or are under stress. Basically a description of the average modern lifestyle.

Vitamin C supplements are pretty much essential for most of us and do more than just help prevent colds in winter. Many of the beneficial effects of this vitamin are in fact the effects of vitamin C and a group of substances always found together with it in nature: the bioflavonoids. They have powerful effects on blood capillaries and have an even greater beneficial effect on scurvy, for instance, than purified vitamin C. Bioflavonoids are also potent free radical fighters. Vitamin C together with bioflavonoids form a powerful team against ageing. This increase in effectiveness from combined factors happens all the time in nature and is called 'synergy'. This is why you will still benefit from adding raw fruit and vegetables to your diet. And, of course, herbs. Many factors found in nature will keep you young. Bioflavonoids, by the way, are found in the pith of citrus fruits in good concentrations. Red onions are high in quercetin which is also a flavonoid and has remarkable anti-oxidant power. It is very beneficial in the treatment of varicose veins.

It is important to use *enough* vitamin C when you are looking for a good response during critical times. The bioflavonoids are easily obtained if you eat the pith of one or two oranges each day and if you add dark-coloured berries to your diet, as well as some raw beetroot or carrots. Vitamin C can then be added even in its synthetic form, as ascorbic acid. I have found that to be the most effective form of vitamin C but many people find it too acidic and for them many 'buffered' forms of the vitamin exist. They are made by combining a mineral with vitamin C. You can choose from magnesium ascorbate, calcium ascorbate, zinc ascorbate and potassium ascorbate. The advantage in using buffered products is that the pH balance of the product is closer to neutral which means it will not irritate your digestive system. Also you get two for the price of one – the mineral as well as the vitamin C. Another form of vitamin C is Ester-C but this one is not as effective as ascorbic acid in my experience. People with kidney disease need to be careful about potassium supplementation and should avoid potassium ascorbate. Magnesium in large amounts can cause diarrhoea and is not desirable – don't exceed one teaspoon of magnesium ascorbate powder per day.

If you are using over 500 mg of vitamin C per day, add three to five drops (15–25 mg) of VitaSorb B12 to your supplement programme. Leave at least four hours between the two vitamins. Very high doses of vitamin C (over 30–50 grams per day) over many months *may* cause immunosuppression in people who are not seriously ill. For normal, everyday use I recommend 500 mg of vitamin C each day, plus VitaSorb C directly on the face. If you have a chronic condition such as asthma or a food allergy, this amount of vitamin C, together with avoidance or complete elimination of dairy foods and, if possible, of animal products, ought to produce marked relief in your condition. If you become ill with a cold, flu or a chest infection you can safely use three to six grams (one gram is a thousand milligrams) of vitamin C per day and return to your normal maintenance dosage when you have recovered.

For any disease involving the respiratory organs, always remember to add beta carotene to your vitamin regime (see later). Recently there have also been suggestions that vitamin C could lead to kidney stones. These concerns are unfounded in healthy people. If you suffer from kidney disease obtain the advice of a health professional you can trust before taking any supplements. Don't forget that if you were eating a 'wild' diet, largely composed of fruit as our ancestors did, you would be getting somewhere between six and thirty grams of vitamin C per day! Your body needs it and basically has no problem handling even very large amounts of it. But find your own personal balance and take advice if worried.

Now let's see what vitamin C can do for your looks. For youthfulness, vitamin C strengthens collagen. Collagen is the substance which gives your skin firmness and support. Support is what your skin needs after thirty-five and even before. I suggest you use one gram of ascorbic acid or its equivalent, together with regular nightly application of VitaSorb C to your face, neck and hands, to strengthen the tissues. The results are, happily, quite fast.

Vitamin C is incredibly effective at stimulating the production of interferon which means that it deactivates many viruses and also works against bacterial invasion. This vitamin plays a great role in protecting you from the effects of pollution and the chemicals used by the food industry and fruit and vegetable growers. It minimises the effects of carbon monoxide, cadmium, mercury, lead, copper, arsenic, benzene and some pesticides. It also prevents the formation of harmful nitrosamines from nitrites and nitrates which are found in many commercially produced foods, especially smoked foods and sausages.

The heart loves vitamin C and, of course, a healthy heart is essential for a long life. This vitamin also has a calming effect on the nervous system and this enhances its beneficial effect on the heart. Vitamin C greatly stimulates your entire immune system and both protects against and can help cure cancer. Large doses (for example five or even ten grams per day) will be needed to reverse a condition such as cancer and I would strongly recommend an intensive programme which includes the correct Chinese herbs, as well as plenty of beta carotene, selenium, magnesium and the B complex. Vitamin C can regulate thyroid function and stimulates your body to produce heat. Some athletes have used it to build muscle tone. Many people complaining of feeling tired and described as 'anaemic' despite their intake of iron-rich foods such as meat and eggs often find that iron supplements don't help at all. Vitamin C can work wonders for these people. Believe it or not, cayenne pepper is also a great pick-me-up tonic which stimulates your immune system – make sure it's not cooked, though. If you want strong teeth well into old age, make sure you get plenty of vitamin C. Silicon from horsetail herb is another important element in the tooth programme. As you can see, vitamin C is much more than just a cold cure.

Some of the most remarkable effects of vitamin C come when it is used in very high doses, almost like a pharmaceutical substance. These doses are still within normal physiological requirements, however, if calculated with respect to animals which manufacture the vitamin in their bodies according to need. For example, taking just fourteen grams of vitamin C for several days can protect you against fatal doses of mercury and the same dose could protect you against oxygen deprivation. The mechanism for the latter is unknown but it does point to some impressive protective actions of this vitamin. Protection which will certainly enhance the efficiency of your whole body.

Vitamin C is found in particularly high concentrations in the lungs, where there are high levels of oxygen and, therefore, high potential levels of free radicals. Similarly vitamin C is concentrated in the brain to protect the neurotransmitters against free radical damage. In this way vitamin C improves brain functioning and can even help in cases of memory loss. For the best results, however, it is necessary to combine vitamin C with the other two anti-oxidant vitamins, beta carotene and vitamin E. Even better, add selenium, Ginkgo Biloba, bioflavonoids from berries, Dang Gui which enhances vitamin E utilisation and chaparral which has remarkable anti-oxidant properties of its own. More of these later. For now, let's explore the benefits of the other anti-oxidant vitamins.

Beta Carotene

Applied externally either in the form of carrot juice or as a spirulina pack, or taken as a vitamin dissolved in water, beta carotene has great anti-ageing potential. The trouble is that it is yellow, or, in the case of spirulina, one of the best sources of beta carotene, *very* green. It washes off, however, so do try it externally anyway, but protect your clothing. Some of the liquid beta carotene preparations will have to be removed with oil and tissues if used externally and do stain, so it's best to avoid them. Internally beta carotene is a veritable fountain of youth. It is converted to vitamin A and this vitamin itself is great for the skin. Beta carotene is, however, non-toxic, unlike the fat soluble vitamin A. Beta carotene is also a very potent free radical scavenger. It has been shown to protect smokers against lung cancer. Beta carotene also protects DNA from attack by free radicals. This makes it a major defence against both cancer and ageing.

I recommend you use the following dose in your rejuvenation programme: 7500 i.u. per day, which can be doubled or tripled during an illness, especially one which involves the respiratory system. If your product is marked in milligrams, 15 mg is a good basic dose which can be doubled or tripled in times of need. Beta carotene can clear a runny nose very quickly if you make sure you are not making things worse by eating animal products. Also remember beta carotene if you ever get a urinary infection. In this case, add some cranberry powder or sugar-free cranberry juice. BioCare produce two good cranberry products. The wonderful beta carotene can also protect your skin from sun damage both by minimising the effects of free radical damage and by enhancing the production of melanin which acts as a skin barrier against the sun.

Vitamin E

In many ways this is the darling of the cosmetics world; it protects your skin very powerfully against free radicals, being particularly potent against sun damage. It will even *repair* skin damaged by the sun – for this take it both internally in the morning and use it externally each night. Vitamin E also keeps your skin cells moist and prevents the development of lines (the dreaded wrinkle!). It has great affinity for the heart and circulation, stops the formation of blood clots, prevents and treats varicose veins, benefits certain types of sterility and, above all, may well have the ability to delay the ageing of your cells and make you look young for longer. For example, the red blood cells of people who had received vitamin E supplements aged far less than the cells of people who had not received vitamin E. When human cells were grown in the presence of extra vitamin E they lived longer than cells grown without this extra dose. Vitamin E is particularly potent as an anti-oxidant which prevents the oxidation of polyunsaturated fatty acids and so maintains the strength and integrity of cellular membranes. If you combine the external application of this vitamin to wrinkled areas with internal supplementation you will not only greatly decrease the cross-linking which results in wrinkles from the inside but also you will be affecting the formation of the skin cells in the outer layer of your skin, giving a healthy, pink glow to your complexion. Vitamin E is also excellent at reversing and stopping the gradual decline in metabolic rate which so often accompanies ageing. It will stop thinning hair and it will keep your sex organs in peak condition. It can also be applied to burns, where it will heal tissue and prevent scarring, and when applied to old scars will dissolve scar tissue. Animals that were given vitamin E supplements had a reduced death rate and a longer life span. Vitamin E greatly increases stamina and performance of athletes and racehorses, too! It also perks up the immune system and can give protection against viral diseases – a bit like a vaccine without side-effects. Vitamin E is a very potent factor for keeping your body looking and feeling young. If you decide to try just one vitamin against ageing, make it E.

The B Complex

The group of vitamins that makes up the B complex is necessary for the proper metabolism of fat, carbohydrate and protein. These vitamins are also essential for the proper functioning of the nervous system and for the maintenance of skin, hair, eyes, mouth and liver. Our diets are generally so poor that almost everybody lacks the B complex boost. Grey, falling hair, poor muscle tone, skin which has uneven colouring with red patches and skin which burns in the sun are all indicative of B vitamin deficiency. Nervous people and people under stress have an increased need for these vitamins and the B complex can improve your thinking powers too. It has proved helpful in cases of senile dementia. Improvement has been noted in as little as twenty-four hours.

Now let's look at this family of vitamins in more detail. Remember, the way to take them is together not separately. Make sure that the vitamins B1, B2, B3, B4, B5 and B6 are all supplied in the same quantities, for example, all at 25 mg.

VITAMIN B1 – THIAMINE

This one gives a woman Great Attitude. You can be strong and calm, bright and self-assured. Serious deficiencies of B1 will lead to symptoms of paranoia, manic-depressive illness and the loss of emotional control, while smaller deficiencies will make you argument-ative, irritable and tired.

Thiamine, together with B3 and B6, has been used in the treatment of multiple sclerosis and, together with a multi-vitamin programme, in myasthenia gravis. I would recommend this regime accompanied by high doses of vitamin E which Dr Abram Hoffer has used successfully in Huntington's chorea, and I would also add herbs such as Ling Zhi, Siberian ginseng, He Shou Wu, Gou Qi Zi and Schizandra to intensify the treatment.

Thiamine is essential in the manufacture of hydrochloric acid, levels of which decline with age which is probably linked more to a prolonged deficiency of vitamins such as thiamine than to an inherent and necessary decrease in production caused by chronological ageing. Thiamine can also be used to alleviate nausea, especially when caused by motion sickness.

VITAMIN B2 – RIBOFLAVIN

Remember this famous cure for red eyes, especially after alcohol. It can also correct hair loss. Tense, underweight people derive great benefit from supplementation with this vitamin, which will help to bring their weight up to normal levels. If your eyes are sensitive to the sun, if you have a 'gritty' feeling like sand in your eyes, you need riboflavin. In fact, these conditions are early indications of a possibility of cataracts, so don't ignore them. Riboflavin has been very useful as a treatment for cataracts as well.

VITAMIN B3 – NIACIN, NICOTINIC ACID, NIACINAMIDE, NICOTINAMIDE

A remarkable anti-ageing substance as well as a remarkably potent detoxifying agent. It has been used in detox programmes all over the world, helping to remove Agent Orange residues in Vietnam veterans as well as detoxifying bodies from heroin, alcohol and anti-depressants. In many cases of senile dementia it has been invaluable. For RR purposes the niacin form of B3 is preferable although the nicotinamide will be effective as an anti-ageing substance if it is started early enough, in your thirties or forties rather than your sixties. The later you begin supplementation the more you will need niacin rather than nicotinamide. Always use a high-potency B complex rather than an individual B vitamin when supplementing your diet with these vitamins. Should you wish to use individual B vitamins for a special purpose such as detoxification, you may add this vitamin on top of your high-potency supplement. However, consult a health practitioner if you wish to use very high doses of any vitamin. Nicotinamide is also very effective for cancer prevention; it works by regulating an enzyme which protects normal cells from becoming malignant.

Niacin is very effective at dilating blood vessels which is why it causes the characteristic flush when taken in doses over 50 mg in one go. It has provided arthritis sufferers with relief and has also helped insomniacs sleep. It has such a tremendously powerful calming effect that many people have used it instead of tranquillisers. Niacin has been used in the treatment of alcoholics and as a fast method to minimise the hallucinogenic effects of LSD and mescaline. It is a useful treatment for gum infections such as pyorrhoea, which, left untreated, may cause tooth loss. Acne also responds very well to supplementation with this vitamin. Even Parkinson's disease has been helped by niacin. In a disease such as Parkinson's all of the anti-oxidant vitamins and minerals should be used.

VITAMIN B5 – PANTHOTHENIC ACID

Roger Williams, the discoverer of this vitamin, postulated that if supplementation with pantothenic acid began in childhood, the expected life span could be increased by ten years. And that's just one single vitamin! Pantothenic acid is found in high concentrations in royal jelly, the food which is the sole nourishment of the queen bee, extending her life span from a few weeks to three years. It works for mice, too, increasing their life expectancy.

Pantothenic acid is closely related to the functioning of the adrenal glands and so plays an essential role in coping with stress, after injury, during severe or prolonged illness or following antibiotic therapy. Vitamin B5 shares many functions with its other vitamin B cousins; it is useful for eye problems, including cataracts, important for nerve function, skin and muscle disorders and very good for improving the condition of the hair. It will also greatly boost your energy levels within minutes of taking it together with the whole B complex regime.

VITAMIN B6 – PYRIDOXINE

The best supplemental form of this vitamin is pyridoxal-5-phosphate. Pyridoxine deficiency is associated with many nerve complaints, particularly the sort of pain which afflicts shoulders, hands, wrists and fingers, one of which, known as the carpal tunnel syndrome, is entirely reversible and *curable* with B complex supplementation, even though many nurses and midwives, who see a lot of this syndrome, still state categorically that nothing can be done apart from surgery. (I do not, however, recommend taking pyridoxine on its own.) Painful knots and spurs on the side of finger joints, something which afflicts menopausal women and elderly men, can be dramatically improved with supplementation of this vitamin. B6 has also brought some rather unexpected and beneficial effects in Parkinson's disease, but for this purpose it needs to be given by injection. It is also very effective in the treatment of pre-menstrual tension, especially when accompanied by bloating and irritability. If you don't have vivid dreams and if you don't remember your dreams you are probably deficient in this vitamin. A common cause of B6 deficiency is the contraceptive pill. This can produce far-reaching deficiencies lasting many years beyond the actual time of medication. It is therefore very important to take supplements of the known vulnerable vitamins at least, while you are on the pill. These are described at the end of this section.

VITAMIN B12

This vitamin is fascinating because it contains cobalt, a mineral, because it is vital for longevity and because it is often quoted as being available from animal sources only, thus inciting great controversy about its levels and availability in plant material. B12 is, in fact, present in non-animal sources, most notably blue-green algae such as spirulina, chlorella and the algae from Lake Klamath. Spirulina and chlorella also contain B12 analogues, however, which may or may not interfere with the function of B12 in the body. Scientifically speaking, this is still an unresolved question. But people who have used spirulina as a source of B12 over many years have shown no deficiency symptoms. Typically, B12 deficiency does not show up for many years and may be masked (or even compensated) by a high intake of folic acid, a vitamin which is widespread in plant foods and would, therefore, be plentiful in the diet of the very people who are often told to be careful about their intake of B12. However, recent evidence suggests that a deficiency of B12 is often caused by a lack of an 'intrinsic factor' responsible for its absorption rather than a simple lack of B12 in the diet. This view appears to be substantiated by the finding that many meat eaters are B12 deficient even though they consume diets which should provide them with plenty of B12. Of course, animal products are usually eaten cooked which means that most of the vitamin is destroyed.

Having studied the literature, used both chlorella and spirulina over several years and spoken with people who have a good deal of experience with these algae, I consider both spirulina and chlorella to be very valuable and safe superfoods and useful as B12 sources. Lake Klamath algae would be an even better choice. Other sources of B12 are seaweeds and fermented foods, but make sure they are raw. Your own bacteria in the intestines and the mouth are probably the best sources of B12. However, if you are at all worried, take two or three drops of VitaSorb B12 every day. It is available from BioCare.

From the point of view of rejuvenation it is interesting to note that vitamin B12 is crucial for protein, fat and carbohydrate metabolism, is necessary for healthy nerve function and, most interesting of all, aids in the production of DNA and RNA, the body's genetic material. RNA and DNA are completely essential for life. The more efficient your production of RNA and DNA the better you'll look and the longer you will be around to keep smiling! B12 will also help you keep your bones strong and is useful in the treatment of obesity.

The best form of vitamin B12 to look for in supplements is hydroxy-cobalamin rather than cyano-cobalamin. The levels required by the body are very small – they are measured in micrograms (one-millionth of a gram), not milligrams.

PABA – PARA-AMINO-BENZOIC ACID

Para-amino-benzoic acid is extremely important for skin health and skin tone, for hair colour (as in keeping it and not going grey) and even gives a good degree of sun protection both as an external sunscreen and when taken internally. There have even been cases of people's hair regaining its natural colour after they had gone grey when they were given supplements of PABA. For this purpose combine it with He Shou Wu if you can and make sure you are taking all of the B complex vitamins, particularly folic acid, which works together with PABA to reverse greying hair.

A GOOD B COMPLEX SUPPLEMENT

A good balanced B complex capsule should look like this:

Vitamin B1 50 mg
Vitamin B2 50 mg
Vitamin B3 (nicotinamide) 50 mg
Vitamin B5 (pantothenic acid) 50 mg
Vitamin B6 (pyridoxal-5-phosphate) 50 mg
PABA 30 mg
Choline 30 mg
Inositol 30 mg
Folic acid 400 mcg (micrograms)
Biotin 200 mcg
Vitamin B12 (hydroxy-cobalamin) 50 mcg

For everyday use, half of the above capsule taken in a little water is sufficient. Or you could take one whole capsule for a month if you are particularly run-down and then halve it at the end of this time when you feel on the mend.

In these modern times supplements are our allies for combating a toxic chemical onslaught. Many of us also rely on more chemicals for relaxation. Cigarettes and alcohol, for example. Women are particularly vulnerable to imbalance caused by chemicals because their bodies undergo such profound changes not just once a month but throughout a life time, especially if the woman has had children. The contraceptive pill has brought freedom to many women but at a cost – it greatly disturbs the function of a woman's body. One recent survey has shown that natural fertility planning, such as the Billings method, when practised correctly and responsibly, has a success rate of protection as high as the pill. Still, many women opt for the pill and, for them, a list of vitamins known to be detrimentally affected by the pill is important. A regular addition of these vitamins to your daily programme can minimise the effects of the pill. Some of the problems caused by this form of contraception include the possibility of varicose veins and thrombosis which may not manifest until later in life and a possible interruption of normal fertility. The pill destroys these vitamins in your body:

Folic acid
B6 – pyridoxine
B2 – riboflavin
B12 – hydroxy-cobalamin
Vitamin E

Make sure you also supplement your diet with extra vitamin C, zinc and a multi-vitamin. However, vitamin C reduces the effectiveness of the pill, so do not use doses higher than 250 mg per day and if you're at all concerned do not supplement with vitamin C. On the other hand, large doses of vitamin C after you have stopped taking the pill will help your body clear it from your tissues.

MINERALS

Now for minerals. I get so excited about what minerals can do against ageing that every time I think of it I have to take a cold shower! I LOVE MINERALS. I've found that, applied to skin and hair as well as taken internally, they can really make you look *very good*! External applications of minerals and vitamins, too, for that matter, together with a raw food diet rich in natural minerals and vitamins, plus the supplements suggested in this book, can literally transform the structure of your skin and hair cells, increasing structural integrity, elasticity and tensile strength. Minerals play a vital role in enzyme function, glucose utilisation, the conversion of amino acids into muscle tissue, and the way your body handles fat. All in all, they are pretty important RR supplements. Let's look at the benefits that minerals can deliver.

Sulphur

Probably my favourite mineral because when you could count the total hair strands on my head in just a little over three seconds sulphur turned it all around. If you want hair, eat sulphur. Not any old sulphur, of course, but Organic Sulphur. This product is easily assimilated and doesn't smell; it's quite different from flowers of sulphur or inorganic sulphur which, when taken internally, can produce an unpleasant body odour.

Sulphur is a non-metallic element which is widely distributed in nature and makes up about quarter of one per cent of the human body weight. Although it has a wide distribution, only very small amounts are actually available to us from our diet. In its most concentrated and bio-available form it is found in breast milk, eggs, garlic, onions and very fresh produce which has not been processed.

One of sulphur's important roles is linked with protein. There are four sulphur-containing amino acids: methionine, cysteine, cystine and taurine. Sulphur plays an essential role in collagen synthesis and is a vital constituent of keratin, a strong structural protein necessary for healthy nails, skin and hair. No wonder sulphur has been called the 'beauty' mineral.

Sulphur is also involved in the proper functioning of your metabolism and the nervous system. It is closely linked with healthy liver function and plays a vital part in tissue respiration, helping to build new cells and release energy. It is also an excellent pollution protector both on its own and as part of the sulphur-containing amino acids.

Clinically, sulphur has been found to be useful in arthritis, dermatitis, eczema and psoriasis. It can be taken internally, in the form of Organic Sulphur, as well as applied directly to the affected area of the skin. External application to the face will produce an immediate tightening and freshening effect which does not, however, lead to any adverse drying.

Earlier in the book we saw the magical effects sulphur has on hair, applied directly on to wet or dry hair.

Silicon

Another of my favourites and another structure builder and strengthener. And, sadly, another mineral all too often deficient in our diets. All the connective tissues in our bodies, such as tendons and cartilage, also blood vessels, skin and bones, contain silicon. Without this mineral bones become soft and deformed, tooth enamel weakens and is prone to decay, skin sags and varicose veins can occur. Silicon is another mineral essential for the formation of healthy, strong collagen. It is also able to antagonise the actions of mercury in your body and is responsible for its safe excretion. Mercury is a poison found in chimney smoke, fish, pesticides, dental fillings and even some vaccines such as the DPT vaccine given to babies. Adequate silicon (as well as selenium, as we shall see) plays a huge part in making this toxic substance less dangerous to your body. Silicon is also essential for people who are sociable, always on the go and periodically drive themselves to a standstill.

Clinically, silicon is useful in treating arteriosclerosis and arthritis. Actually, what is used is horsetail herb (*Equisetum arvense*) which is probably the richest source of this element. Kelp, alfalfa, millet, oats, bee pollen and bell (sweet) peppers also contain the active form of biologically active silicon.

Calcium

To look good and to feel young, your bones and teeth – not just your skin and hair – need to be strong. Ask most people about strong teeth and bones and they'll say calcium. Ask about the sources of calcium and they'll say cheese. So why do we in the West suffer so much from osteoporosis when we eat such heroic quantities of cheese?

Actually, although calcium is important for bone formation it is by no means the only factor responsible for strong bones and teeth, nor is cheese such a good source of bio-available calcium. Osteoporosis is a very interesting case to consider. You only have to look at native African women to appreciate the advantages of having great bones.

Osteoporosis is created by an excess of protein and sugar (and probably an *excess* of calcium because this blocks bone formation by interfering with vitamin D utilisation) and a deficiency of silicon, boron and magnesium. Also very high levels of oestrogen and progesterone as well as an imbalance of the two hormones are important factors in this disease. Those tribal women with wonderful bone structure eat a quarter of the recommended daily amount of calcium and they don't get osteoporosis. Yet Eskimos, who obtain just about the highest amounts of calcium in their diet, even slightly above the recommended level, suffer from this disease. The diet of the African tribal women is low in protein, animal protein in particular, while the Eskimos eat protein primarily of animal origin. This also affects their life expectancy, giving them one of the shortest expectancies of any group of people in the world.

When you know how your body functions diseases stop being a mystery. In the West we have perfected methods for maximising health problems. Luxuries called cigarettes, sugar, alcohol, caffeine, tea and chocolate are responsible for most of them. Sugar is especially brilliant at upsetting the calcium/phosphorus balance, leading to weak bones. Eating chocolate means you are getting rid of magnesium and calcium. Recent research has shown that *all* the minerals in your body are adversely affected by sugar. You can be eating all the mineral supplements you want but if you eat sugar they will do nothing for you at all. Sweetened and pasteurised yogurt and milk are not health foods, no matter what the ads say. They weaken your whole body and they are not a good source of calcium. Many societies in the world do not use, and have never used, such products as a source of calcium, yet their incidence of osteoporosis is much lower than ours.

Adding table salt to your food is another great way to lose calcium and soften your teeth and bones. Using condiments high in sodium, even healthy ones such as tamari, will deplete you of bone-strengthening minerals and lead to bad teeth and soft bones. On the way to cutting down on salt use kelp powder, dulse flakes, garlic, onion, black pepper, chilli powder or salt-free curry powder. You could also try using small amounts of Celtic sea salt, which is higher in magnesium than ordinary table salt, higher even than sea salt.

However, even Celtic sea salt should be used sparingly and only as a temporary aid in giving up salt altogether. A good way to cut down on salt is to use it at the table only, contrary to what is sometimes recommended. Don't cook with it, but add a little to your food just before eating. That way you will taste it more.

Three cups of coffee get rid of forty-five milligrams of calcium from your body and that's not counting other caffeine sources. Scary! Throw it all out and make an art out of drinking expensive water in beautiful bottles, served with a slice of lemon, lime, orange, mango or pineapple. Or go for the best – fresh carrot juice. Delicious, simple, elegant and *rejuvenating*!

Now you know what's coming. The big one! Alcohol and tobacco. Most of us know the detrimental effects these two luxuries have but here are a few more. Cigarettes have a detrimental effect on oestrogen activity, making them a high runner in the development of weak, brittle bones. As if this weren't enough, cadmium, a heavy metal found in cigarette smoke, can cause extensive bone loss. Cigarette smoke is also very high in radioactive compounds; how about polonium-210 and lead-210? And we haven't begun to mention emphysema, lung cancer and heart disease, all of which are associated with cigarette smoking. Buy yourself some sexy clothes or go on a luxury, and I mean luxury, holiday with the money you'll save, or splash out on some essential oils – real treats not just temporary ones!

Chronic alcohol drinkers have extensive bone loss. Even young drinkers can have old bones if they drink enough. As little as two drinks a day is enough to stop your body absorbing essential bone-making minerals. This includes wine or beer as well as the stronger stuff. Think about taking up the pleasures of bottled drinks and juices. Just remember that last hangover, and the one before . . .

Good sources of magnesium are nuts, leafy greens, seeds, soya beans, kelp, dulse, oats and figs. Calcium is found in almonds, sesame seeds, leafy green vegetables (especially broccoli and kale) and soya bean products such as tofu.

Boron

A relatively new kid on the block but if you want fantastic posture, you need some. Believe it or not, great posture is due to great nutrition, far more than standing tall or artificial poses with shoulders back and chest out. If your body is light and supple from the RR Diet you will stand tall without trying or even thinking.

Boron may well be the most important mineral for the prevention of osteoporosis. In a study of post-menopausal women just three milligrams of boron a day reduced calcium excretion by forty per cent and increased oestrogen levels in the blood. Such an increase helps prevent bone loss. In addition boron is essential for the production of active vitamin D, and therefore necessary for proper bone formation. What's more, boron also improves the metabolism of calcium, phosphorus and magnesium and decreases calcium, magnesium and oestrogen loss. Recent findings suggest that the link between oestrogen and bone strength is not a simple linear one and that what matters even more is the balance of oestrogen and progesterone. Levels of these two hormones should be steady and not excessive. Women in healthier societies than ours have much lower levels of both oestrogen and progesterone, with smaller deviations in their levels prior to periods, for instance. A diet rich in raw foods and fresh vegetables, fruit and sprouted seeds such as sunflower or alfalfa goes a long way towards balancing hormone levels. *Balance* is the key word here. A balanced body functions at a much higher level of efficiency, utilising the nutrients available from the diet much more effectively and absorbing most of what is eaten. This is not possible with a diet high in animal and cooked foods.

Some good sources of boron are apples, grapes, spinach, alfalfa and kelp.

Magnesium

Magnesium, which is essential for bone strength, works in balance with calcium and is important for energy, is often in short supply in Western diet. It has been found to be extremely effective in treating Chronic Fatigue Syndrome and many other conditions characterised by extreme lack of energy. It is also necessary for the proper functioning of many enzymes involved in the breakdown of sugar in the liver, a process which creates energy. Magnesium has also been found to be essential during pregnancy; adequate levels of this mineral will avoid many complications, including pre-eclampsia, prematurity and intra-uterine growth retardation. I have also found vitamin E to be a useful supplement in pregnancy that will increase foetal growth rate if it is suboptimal. If you are pregnant or thinking about conceiving a baby, however, always consult a health expert before taking anything, even vitamins. Magnesium is wonderful for babies who cry a lot and for anxious grown-ups too. A long-term deficiency of magnesium will eventually show up as senility, lack of mental clarity, anxiety, twitching or muscle tremors and blood clots.

Zinc

As we have seen in the chapter on skin, zinc stands for super skin. It is vital for the synthesis of RNA and DNA, both of them great skin dynamos. It is also essential for protein synthesis and to maintain adequate levels of vitamin A in the blood. All of these are already famous anti-wrinklers. Further, zinc is a constituent of at least twenty-five enzymes which play a role in digestion and metabolism, including carbonic anhydrase, which is involved in tissue respiration. Recently zinc has been shown to be essential for the healing of wounds and burns. It will also prevent stretch marks in pregnancy or those due to excessive weight. If you suffer from sleeplessness, 7–15 mg of zinc at bedtime will work wonders. Zinc is found in ginger root, pecan nuts, almonds, walnuts, hazelnuts, brazil nuts, pumpkin seeds, cabbage, spinach, lettuce, carrots, cucumbers and tangerines.

Some health food shops now sell a do-it-yourself kit which you can use to see if you are low in zinc and in need of supplemental doses. Do not use supplements over 30 mg daily without consulting a nutritionist or GP.

Potassium

If your skin is dry, if your muscles lack tone and if you don't eat much in the way of fruit and vegetables, you would benefit from potassium. It is involved in cell metabolism, enzyme function and protein metabolism and it enables your body to use fatty acids efficiently, making a sort of 'soap' out of them. Insufficient potassium means that fats are not utilised properly by the body, resulting in painful joints and rheumatism. Excessive salt intake which produces high blood pressure can be treated by potassium. Twenty-five to 50 mg is a good supplemental dose. Also include some potassium-containing food in your diet. Kelp, dulse, sunflower seeds, almonds, raisins, peanuts, dates, avocados, figs, bananas, carrots and papaya are all high in potassium. One of the best potassium supplements is potassium ascorbate which is vitamin C (ascorbic acid) buffered, that is, made less acidic, by the addition of potassium. But it should not be taken by people with kidney disease.

Selenium

Selenium is vital for young-looking skin. It makes your skin supple and elastic by protecting it (and the rest of you) from free radical damage by delaying oxidation of polyunsaturated fatty acids. Selenium protects you against cancer, is essential for male fertility, protects the heart and has been used clinically to reduce or eliminate angina attacks. Since it is necessary for the production of protaglandins it will normalise blood pressure. It has also been found to be an excellent mood enhancer and effective at speeding up the metabolic rate. Both selenium and zinc are necessary for the synthesis of glutathione peroxidase and superoxide dismutase (SOD). Without these two minerals your body simply cannot make these two enzymes. However, both selenium and zinc can have detrimental effects if used in high dosages. Zinc, for example, vital for immune function, will actually *suppress* immunity if taken in *too* high a dose (more than 30 mg of elemental zinc) over several weeks. Seven to 15 mg daily of elemental zinc is a safe dose. Selenium can be quite toxic in certain forms and not so in others. One of the safest forms of selenium is selenomethionine. A hundred micrograms (a microgram is one thousand times smaller than a milligram) is a good, safe daily dose.

Selenium is found in brazil nuts, pecans, almonds, mushrooms, garlic, cabbage, carrots, oranges, grapes and hazelnuts, provided that the soil in which these foods grew contained the mineral. And this is the problem with modern farming methods – exhausted and 'bad' soil. Minerals are in such short supply in our diets we could all benefit from supplemental doses. For the sake of a youthful body and mind make sure you get your minerals.

In this chapter we have looked at some exciting things that minerals can do for your beauty and rejuvenation. Here are some suggestions on the best forms of minerals available and when to take them for best effects. The old inorganic forms of minerals can be difficult for your body to utilise; such inactive compounds include mineral oxides, chlorides and sulphates. They are difficult for the body to digest and absorb and create more problems than benefits when ingested. If you follow my guidelines, however, you will reap the rewards of using minerals for Radical Rejuvenation.

Mineral Guidelines

SULPHUR

The best form of sulphur is methylsulphonylmethane (MSM) sold under the name Organic Sulphur. One to three capsules per day taken with breakfast is a good dose. Pour the contents of a capsule into a small amount of water.

The sulphur-containing amino acids such as cysteine or methionine are another possibility for taking sulphur. But you have to be careful because many of these amino acids are derived from animal products such as milk and I do not recommend those. BioCare products can be trusted. Their Amino-Plex will provide you with a good dose of cysteine, methionine and lysine, delivering a useful dose of sulphur along the way. Take one to three capsules at breakfast as above.

SILICON

Occurs naturally as organic silica. The best bio-available supplement of this essential mineral is found in the herb horsetail (*Equisetum arvense*). I usually take one teaspoon of the powdered herb in the morning and it really does strengthen your nails and hair fast. You can combine it with an equal amount of marshmallow root powder to soothe the effect of horsetail on the kidneys. Stir into a small amount of water and drink. It does look very green but it tastes rather nice, I think. But then I am a herb fanatic!

CALCIUM AND MAGNESIUM

These minerals work together and are best taken together, either in the EAP2 form, as Calcium EAP2 and Magnesium EAP2 or as Mag 2:1 Cal, all from BioCare. Go for 100 mg of magnesium and calcium. Don't worry about the ratio of magnesium to calcium too much; some people recommend 2:1 but there is much debate on the subject. One hundred milligrams of each is a good basis for healthy bones and nerves. Double the dose if you suffer from excessive fatigue (magnesium is the one for this) but if you want to increase it beyond this consult a health expert. I took much greater amounts than this while I was pregnant and my baby was born beautiful and healthy, but do seek professional advice if you wish to take supplements in high doses, *especially* if you think you may be pregnant or if you are lactating.

BORON

Three to six milligrams a day is safe. It is best combined with magnesium and calcium. Personally I rely on apples as a good source of this mineral. In this respect three to four apples a day should do it. Pears and grapes are also rich in this mineral.

POTASSIUM

One capsule of potassium ascorbate from BioCare will provide you with 41 mg of potassium and nearly half a gram of vitamin C. Don't forget to eat bananas, dates, figs, avocados, kelp, dulse, almonds, raisins, brazil nuts and peanuts, too. If you suffer from swollen ankles you should notice a difference when increasing potassium in your diet. Decrease table salt at the same time for best results. However, if you have a medical condition, do obtain professional advice before taking supplemental potassium.

ZINC

This one is best taken at bedtime, at least an hour or so after food and longer if possible. Zinc citrate is a good form of the mineral. Seven milligrams a day is a good maintenance dose. High doses (over 30 mg per day for several weeks) are not recommended and can cause immunosuppression. Again consult a health professional to get the right dose for you. We are all individuals so remember to get the right balance for you. And this goes for all the supplements.

SELENIUM

This mineral illustrates very clearly the difference between various forms of mineral supplements. For example, sodium selenite is more toxic than selenomethionine. Selenomethionine is sold under the name Organic Selenium. One hundred micrograms a day is a good dose. Take it together with vitamin E, 200 i.u. If you are taking beta carotene and vitamin C take them all together. Morning is best for these.

RR IN ACTION

A man in his twenties had a stomach ulcer. It was causing him a great deal of pain and on two occasions he had to have a blood transfusion. Conventional drug treatment had failed to resolve his problem. When I met him he was very thin and tired. He was willing to try an alternative approach to the treatment he had been receiving. I advised him to broaden his diet to try and build him up a little – in order to avoid discomfort he had been eating almost nothing. Although I gave him a strong, supportive programme of vitamins and minerals, including iron, the most important part of his treatment was EnteroPlex, a product made by BioCare. It contains deglycyrrhizinated liquorice (DGL). This form of liquorice does not have aldosterone-like effects and so does not cause a rise in sodium and blood pressure. It is, however, a highly effective anti-ulcer agent. In a matter of weeks the man reported far less discomfort after eating. Within months he looked and felt much better. A year later the condition had cleared up, he had taken up martial arts training, had a girl friend and seemed very happy.

CHAPTER NINE

Herbs

You are about to meet some of the most powerful anti-ageing agents in the world – so hold on to your hat! They are more complex and more potent than any commercial synthetic supplement could ever be, although the supplements, too, have their unique power. Herbs often produce their effects quietly; you feel and look much better but this seems somehow to come from within you, so often you don't realise that the herbs have helped you. But there are other times when the effects are unmistakably beneficial, especially in the case of someone who is particularly run-down or suffering from a very debilitating illness such as cancer, ME or multiple sclerosis. I have witnessed the most remarkable, miraculous healing which can only be attributed to the use of these herbs. However, remember that if you have an acute disease such as a cold or influenza, particularly if a fever is present, do *not* use the herbs described in this chapter; they can drive the disease further into your body and make you worse. Specific herbs for the treatment of colds, coughs and flu are appropriate and effective in the treatment of these acute disorders. Also, remember that if you are pregnant or breast feeding you should not take *anything* unless it is essential. Always consult a professional before you use essential oils, take herbs or other supplements if you are expecting a baby or if you are breast feeding.

The herbs in question form part of a group of plants which exert an astonishing effect on the human body – that of bringing the whole system into balance. *Balance*, that word again, a key factor in RR. In this way an illness is cured without any need to suppress symptoms. In many herbal traditions such herbs have occupied a very special place; they were known as the 'royal herbs' in ancient China and widely used by the Taoists who were famous for their longevity; in India they were called 'rasayana' and also used to increase life span and for rejuvenation; in the West they are known as 'tonics'.

Recently the division between Western and Eastern herbs has been getting narrower. Powerful herbs grow all over the world. My aim is to introduce you to the most beneficial, most easily accessible and most economical herb rejuvenators. Dang Gui, for example, is better than Western angelica; Korean ginseng is good, even when it is not of the highest quality. American ginseng is probably as good as and possibly better (it is not as 'hot') than much of the Korean ginseng but it's harder to find in the UK. The following list of herbs is, therefore, deliberately not arranged according to area of origin. It's really an 'inside-out' sort of list. The herbs which open the chapter are some of the most useful substances for Radical Rejuvenation in terms of both performance and cost to be found anywhere; this is why herbs such as

He Shou Wu and Schizandra appear first – they are cheap (especially if you buy them in bulk from mail order firms such as East-West Herbs or the Herbal Apothecary; the tinctures are easily available from Neal's Yard Apothecary) and they are supreme rejuvenators. Ginseng, being relatively expensive, is mentioned a little later in the chapter. It is a wonderful rejuvenator without a doubt but you can replace it with the cheaper herbs if you wish.

Here are my favourite herbs for Radical Rejuvenation:

HE SHOU WU (*POLYGONUM MULTIFLORUM*)

As we saw in Chapter One this one's a real star and my dearest herb. Removes wrinkles, restores grey hair to its original colour, is rumoured to regrow teeth and increase life span – and it is one of the best aphrodisiacs. The oldest roots are of the highest quality. A fifty-year-old root will preserve the colour of your hair, a hundred-year-old root will make your face look young; a hundred-and-fifty-year-old root is supposed to be able to make you grow new teeth (if you need them that is)! Presumably much older roots have even greater powers of rejuvenation. I have certainly seen the roots restore grey hair to its original colour. Look out for the dark roots rather than ones with a lot of white in them. You can buy He Shou Wu in slices, powdered or in tincture form. I usually buy it in a form in which I can mix it with other herbs I like, stir into some water and yippee!

WU WEI ZI (*SCHIZANDRA CHINENSIS*)

This will give you great skin and a great sex life. I love this herb, especially in tincture form. The part used medicinally is the fruit of the plant and tastes quite odd but not unpleasant – it's supposed to have all the five tastes in it: sweet, salty, bitter, sour and pungent. Wu Wei Zi means 'five flavours herb' in Chinese and Schizandra has been highly prized in China for thousands of years. The berries are high in tannin so soak them overnight and throw away the soaking water before using them to make tea. Schizandra gets on well with Gou Qi Zi berries and the two make a tasty tea together or can be mixed as tinctures. Schizandra is comparable to ginseng in producing non-specific resistance to stress, which means stamina, youthfulness and longevity if taken regularly. Herbs for rejuvenation can and should be taken every day for the rest of your life if at all possible. The longer you take them, the more benefit you will derive from them.

Schizandra is used to give men sexual 'staying power' and to increase the woman's sensitivity and responsiveness. If used for a hundred days in succession, Schizandra will markedly increase vitality and give a radiant glow to the skin.

This herb also has a protective effect against liver toxins and is helpful in liver disorders. It has been found to contain immuno-stimulating substances, some of which have cortisone-like effects.

GOTU KOLA (*CENTELLA ASIATICA, HYDROCOTYLE ASIATICA*)

This herb, of which there are many variants, contains steroid-like compounds and has a long, distinguished history as a longevity builder and tranquilliser. It has been used to increase the learning abilities of school children and in the treatment of varicose veins. It has also been extensively used by Indian yogis to improve meditation.

Various studies on rats, mice and guinea pigs have shown that Gotu Kola has a remarkable affinity for the connective tissues and strongly increases the integrity of the dermis which is the support structure of the skin, thus firming and strengthening the tissues and eradicating droops and sags. It has an extremely powerful healing effect on connective tissue, making it very valuable in the treatment of varicose ulcers, varicose veins, cellulite, burns and keloids, which are old, swollen scars consisting of swollen collagen bundles. In addition Gotu Kola has been found to have strongly therapeutic effects in leprosy and scleroderma. Gotu Kola also speeds up the growth of hair and nails. It is hardly surprising, then, to find that this herb figures strongly in many successful youth-restoring and longevity programmes. Gotu Kola has a cholinergic action on the central and peripheral nervous systems. This action on the central nervous system gives it mild tranquillising properties and helps to develop and sharpen mental abilities, even in disabled children. The cholinergic action may also make it a useful substance in the treatment of Huntington's chorea, a disease which is marked by a cholinergic deficit in the basal ganglia of the brain.

Although Gotu Kola does not contain caffeine it has strong energising properties and is often used as a tonic. Oral doses of the dried or powdered herb, in tincture, tea or capsules, have been found to be safe. I suggest a teaspoonful of the powdered herb or tincture, one to three times a day.

ALFALFA (*MEDICAGO SATIVA*)

The green tops of alfalfa, either fresh or dried, are used as a superb tonic for hair, skin, nails and vitality. Alfalfa means 'father of all foods' in Arabic and this herb was also held in high regard and used as a medicine by the Red Indians.

Alfalfa is extremely rich in chlorophyll, silica, beta carotene, octacosanol, bioflavonoids, vitamins (B6, B1, B12, C, E, K, niacin, pantothenic acid, biotin, folic acid), amino acids, minerals (calcium, phosphorus, potassium, magnesium, zinc), trace elements and other nutrients – quite a package.

It builds incredible vitality, is a fantastic liver and kidney tonic, enhances glandular and neuromuscular function, helps the digestive system, can alleviate bloating and is good for the reproductive system too. Traditionally, alfalfa has been one of the best treatments for arthritis, rheumatism and gout. Because it is so rich in chlorophyll it can be used to minimise tissue damage caused by radiation treatment and help to heal scars. By a mechanism as yet unknown to science, plants rich in chlorophyll have substantial renewing and regenerating effects on the human body. There are similarities between chlorophyll and our own respiratory pigment, haemoglobin, even though one is green and the other is red. (There are some respiratory pigments in the human body which are not red.) Whatever the mechanism, the green factor in plants has a remarkably rejuvenating effect on the human organism. People who suffer from auto-immune disorders such as lupus and rheumatoid arthritis should be careful when taking alfalfa. Small amounts, such as one teaspoon of the dried powder or a large spoonful or two of the fresh alfalfa sprouts, should be fine but one study has shown a worsening of symptoms in auto-immune disorders with alfalfa. This is only one study, however, and many people with auto-immune disorders continue to take and benefit from alfalfa. Often negative findings from studies take on a great significance even when poorly carried out and when the results are inconclusive. However, it is fine to be cautious and aware of the possibility of problems in this case.

GINKGO BILOBA

The Ginkgo Biloba tree is ancient – it is believed to pre-date the Ice Age. The trees are believed to be able to live for between two thousand and four thousand years and there are some in existence today which are over one thousand years old. Ginkgo is native to China and Japan but has been cultivated throughout the world and is very resilient. In fact it is resistant to viruses, fungi and pollution.

In Chinese medicine the seeds are used medicinally but they contain toxic principles and are never used in the West. When talking of 'Ginkgo' we mean the leaves of the tree. And don't let anyone tell you that whole, powdered Ginkgo leaf is not effective! Such a powder, when obtained from a reputable herb company and which is therefore not old, is remarkable. The leaves are rich in flavoglycosides and quercetin, a flavonoid. This herb has been found to have significant brain- and liver-protecting properties. It greatly improves blood flow to the brain and has even corrected vision problems, such as myopia.

What all this means is that if you want a young, clear brain, take Ginkgo. It will make you more alert, improve your learning capacity and memory and minimise the possibility of cerebral disorders due to ageing. It may even help in Alzheimer's disease. Disorders of the inner ear, including tinnitus, will also be cured or greatly alleviated by the herb. *And* it is not only a free radical deactivator, it even *prevents* the formation of free radicals and inhibits membrane lipid peroxidation.

GOU QI ZI (*LYCIUM CHINENSIS* OR *LYCIUM BARBARUM*)

Delicious tasting, sweet red berries which give you instant energy, vitality and a sunny disposition. They are extremely high in beta carotene and will improve eyesight and give your eyes a visible sparkle within days. However, this herb is not just a pretty face; it is used in modern Chinese hospitals for nephritis and cancer. Just a handful of Gou Qi Zi berries will raise your mood and energy instantly. Regular use will transform you into a much more cheerful person.

HUANG QI (*ASTRAGALUS MEMBRANACEUS*)

This is a very remarkable root. It has a powerful effect on the thymus gland which was, until recently, thought to be unnecessary in adulthood. Now it is known to play a central role in immunity *and* longevity and youthfulness. Astragalus is a very powerful thymus gland stimulant and regenerator. It has been used after chemotherapy to prevent the considerable damage and atrophy of the thymus gland caused by the chemical treatment. It also greatly protects the lungs against illness and those who take it rarely suffer from colds. This herb also regulates fluid metabolism thus preventing or curing bloating and water retention. Astragalus is also a potent energy tonic, considered by many people to be superior to ginseng.

GINSENG (*REN SHEN, PANAX GINSENG*)

Although Astragalus and all the herbs in the RR programme are undoubtedly wonderful, ginseng is the undisputed reigning King, the one against which all the others are measured. A good ginseng is one of the most potent anti-ageing substances in the world. Problems begin when you try to find a 'good' ginseng in the West. There are some good extracts, however, and some good roots and powders, usually from Korea or Taiwan. The best grade available in the West is usually grade one. True Heaven Grade (three above grade one) is rarely, if ever, available in the West. If you can, use the so-called white rather than the red root. Both types should be raw but they are all routinely steam cleaned. Most of the teas and tablets for sale in health food shops have very little true ginseng activity left. But there are some good products, so shop around. By the way, even an average grade of ginseng will give good results over time. Just increase the dose until you feel you are getting the right result. For instance, if you have a grade three root (East-West Herbs supply grade one) then you need to use three times the dose you'd need of grade one to get the same effect. Three tablets rather than one, for example. Or one and a half teaspoons rather than half.

The most exciting recent findings on ginseng with relevance for rejuvenation centre on its effects on cells. It has been found to greatly prolong the life of cells in culture, enhancing cell proliferation and, excitingly, has been found to have this effect on many types of cells, including those of the liver, the thymus, the skin and the lymphatic system. It also conserves the levels of nerve growth factor which are known to decline with age. It is important to note here that ginseng is the most studied of all herbs, which means that much interesting and impressive evidence exists to support the premise that ginseng is a wonder herb and a great anti-ageing substance.

Ginseng is the pivotal herb in the new class of 'adaptogenic compounds', first described by the Russian pharmacologist I. I. Brekhman. He postulated that an adaptogen is a substance which 1) is harmless, 2) has a non-specific action, that is, it has a wide-ranging effect on the organism by acting on the physical, chemical and biochemical factors in the system. This is an important distinction and makes clear the difference between a specific herb such as peppermint which has a relatively narrow window of activity in the human body and the herbs used in RR such as ginseng and astragalus, all of which are, in fact, adaptogens, which have a tremendously wide range of beneficial action. This is what the Chinese meant by the royal herbs and the Indian sages by rasayana. 3) An adaptogen has a normalising effect, irrespective of the direction of pathology. For example, some people who have taken ginseng found that it lowered their blood pressure, whilst others found that it had the opposite effect. This is because the people in the first group had high blood pressure to start with and those in the second group suffered from low blood pressure. An adaptogen such as ginseng brings both conditions back to normal. Similarly, *Agnus castus*, which some people believe to be an aphrodisiac, while others call it an anaphrodisiac, is simply the same principle in action. It curbs excessive desire which interferes with normal functioning and increases desire whenever a block occurs.

Physical and mental performance is greatly enhanced by the use of ginseng. It produces significant anti-fatigue activity and improves energy metabolism during exercise. It also has quite a remarkable power to help us cope with stress, including emotional and physiological stress, such as extreme cold. Ginseng has also shown protective activity against radiation and this makes it a very important substance in the RR toolkit. Vitamin C deactivates ginseng, however, so don't take them together. Leave eight hours between the two. Also, don't drink anything containing caffeine when you are using ginseng – apart from the fact that caffeine makes you very tense and very anxious, it accentuates the stimulating actions of ginseng and you'll never sleep! The best ginseng for long-term use is Korean white. The red root is considered too 'hot' and is only suitable for short-term, specialised use.

PAU D'ARCO, LAPACHO (*TABEBUIA AVELLANEDAE, TABEBUIA IMPETIGINOSA*)

There are one hundred species of *Tabebuia* native to the tropical regions of South America of which the two named above are the most potent. If you are looking for this plant, make sure it is one of the *Tabebuia* species; some other herbs are erroneously sold under the name LaPacho. One of the active constituents of this plant has been given the name Lapachol. LaPacho is the bark of the Tabebuia tree and the South American Indians generally only use the inner lining of the bark.

LaPacho has the most amazing effects in protecting the human body against disease. It has been found to be highly effective in the treatment of thrush, colds, flu, cancer and psoriasis. It has been used in Parkinson's disease, Hodgkin's disease, lupus, diabetes and osteomyelitis. LaPacho has even been effective as an antidote to poisons. It is a good liver tonic and highly effective against bacterial, fungal and viral infections including a wide range of pathogens, such as *Staphylococcus aureus*, *Candida albicans* and the *Brucella* species. There are many reports of its real anti-cancer activity. So much so that the National Cancer Institute considered it a very promising treatment for cancer and began tests on Lapachol. Unfortunately, one constituent isolated from the complexity of its mother plant is always inferior to the whole complex and these researches found that Lapachol produced nausea due to its anti-vitamin K activity. This problem does *not* occur with the whole plant.

DANG GUI (*ANGELICA CHINENSIS*)

Although the Western angelica root shares some of the properties of Dang Gui, it is better to use the Chinese species. It comes sliced in exotic thin pieces or as a tincture or powder. The root has a smoky, scented taste which I love. Even some children like it.

Dang Gui is called the 'woman's ginseng' in the Orient and it is a wonderful tonic for women. It has strong aphrodisiac properties as well as powerful toning and balancing effects. It has tranquillising actions too and contains phytoestrogens which have an oestrogenic activity in the body. For this reason it should be avoided by women who have heavy periods, as it will make the bleeding worse. It is not necessary to avoid it altogether – simply stop taking it on the first day of your period. Similarly, anyone with an oestrogen-sensitive cancer should avoid the use of angelica species because of the oestrogenic activity. Liquorice is another herb with a strong oestrogenic action.

Dang Gui dilates blood vessels and has a beneficial effect on the cardiovascular system, making it a useful herb against hypertension and angina. It is also good for asthma. Dang Gui is also a very potent pain reliever and can be of help in cramps, especially period pains (in those cases where heavy bleeding is not a problem), trauma, headaches and arthritis. This herb also has anti-bacterial and anti-allergenic properties.

Dang Gui contains coumarins which have been shown to have very potent immune-enhancing activity. They stimulate white blood cells and increase their ability to destroy foreign particles and cancer cells. This offers real protection against the growth of tumours. But anyone with oestrogen-sensitive cancer should keep away from oestrogenic compounds.

When coumarins are taken, specific white blood cells known as macrophages are activated and enter the tumour where they can help to destroy the tumour cells. Water extracts (that is, tea) of both Western and Eastern angelica have been shown to increase the activity of the blood cells, interferon production, anti-tumour activity and the non-specific defence mechanism. So this herb has an important role to play in the treatment of non-oestrogen-sensitive cancers.

The dose for Dang Gui is usually one or two slices of the sliced root preparation, one teaspoon of the powder or a teaspoon of the tincture daily. You may double the dose without any problems. The tincture, especially, since it contains less of the active principle than the herb, may need to be taken in a higher dose. However, this is balanced by the fact that a tincture is absorbed very easily and quickly which gives it a very potent action.

CHAPARRAL (*LARREA MEXICANA, LARREA DIVARICATA*)

Chaparral is also known as the 'Creosote Bush'. You will realise why when you smell the tincture or taste the herb (often tinctures retain and give off a very powerful scent of the mother plant). This herb tastes awful but only in high concentrations. It is also one of my most beloved and respected plants. It is quite easily one of the best protectors of the human body anywhere. It is hundreds, perhaps thousands, of times more effective as an anti-oxidant than the recently acknowledged anti-agers vitamins A (which should properly, though less catchily, be called beta carotene, since it is the beta carotene which carries the anti-oxidant properties, not vitamin A), vitamin C and vitamin E, as well as the slightly less famous selenium. The enzymes in your body are also far more powerful as anti-oxidants than these vitamins, just like the herbs. You do, however, need the vitamins and minerals, not only for their straight physiological role but also in increased doses as anti-oxidants; you need everything to help you stay young in our polluted world.

Chaparral has been described as being good for 'the needy and courageous' because of its taste. I like that description. It is a very strengthening herb and tones the body beautifully. The bitter compounds which give it its famous taste are responsible for a powerful antibiotic action.

Chaparral contains NDGA (nordihydroquaiaretic acid) which has a very strong anti-oxidant action, making it very valuable indeed in the treatment of cancer as well as diseases involving bacterial, viral and parasitic infection. This herb has a strong affinity for the respiratory, urinary and intestinal tracts, clearing infection, inflammation and fever.

Used externally, chaparral will heal wounds, help with eczema, scabies and dandruff and also remove benign cysts and warts if applied directly in a concentrated form such as a tincture. Rinsing your mouth with a diluted form of the tincture (one teaspoon in one mug of water) is effective as prevention against tooth decay.

For use in cancer, chaparral is best combined with equal amounts of red clover and twice as much Pau D'Arco. The usual maintenance dose of chaparral is half a teaspoon of the tincture daily. The tincture is probably easier to take than powder. Add milk thistle seed powder (one teaspoon in juice or water) each time you take chaparral.

Recent reports have given rise to fears that chaparral may occasionally have an adverse effect on the liver. You should consult your practitioner if you are in any way concerned about this. Those with liver or kidney problems are advised not to use chaparral – which can only be obtained through a herbal practitioner.

Herbs are far more complex than any other anti-ageing substance and anything which comes from a laboratory. They are super-foods and super-anti-agers. Even if you have never used herbs for health before try these RR ones – they will help your body stay young for a long time and protect you against disease.

RR IN ACTION

A woman in her fifties was diagnosed as having extensive cancer. It was just about 'everywhere' as she said, including her liver and bones, which is a very frightening picture indeed. Chemotherapy had not produced the desired results and the doctors could do 'no more'. At this point I was consulted. No change in eating was made but a very high quality vitamin and mineral programme was designed, together with a super-herb tincture and powder. This contained many Chinese and Western herbs. Three months later the consultant was heard to remark that the herbs must be miraculous. Over three years later the patient is well, appears to be clear of the disease and has periodic tune-ups with herbs and vitamins. Obviously, the prognosis in such a disease was very bad indeed. It is interesting that the herbs and supplements worked so very well with no change in the patient's diet, though my opinion is that if such changes can be made it can only be good. Another point of interest is that the patient's hair regained its original colour. Prior to the herb therapy it had begun to go grey.

PART THREE

How You Can Make Radical Rejuvenation Work for You

CHAPTER TEN

Diet and Lifestyle

I love food. I've had long love affairs with Big Macs and Galaxy and toasted Mars bars. I used to wake up at six a.m. to catch the newsagent as he first opened for the day – just so that I could eat chocolate for breakfast. And lunch. It showed, believe me. But that wasn't enough to convince me that life without chocolate was possible. If I had been offered a million pounds or even five minutes with Robert Redford instead of my chocolate bar, there wouldn't have been any contest. Nothing and no one tasted as GOOD.

So let me tell you right now that Radical Rejuvenation will *not* rob you of the pleasure of eating. I actually enjoy my food far more now than I ever did when I was in love with chocolate. And I'm not the only one. Just take a peak at the recipes in the following chapter. For lunch today my family had barley cold pot followed by sliced banana with thick cashew nut cream and sweet brazil nut sauce, which is a variation on pecan sauce. Later we had a snack of more sliced banana and almond, cashew and pine kernel cream. For breakfast we often eat avocado slices mixed with chunks of banana. This food is simple to make, simple to eat, delicious and makes you look terrific. And it makes you look younger in a matter of weeks or months. It is also the healthiest diet in the world. This chapter will tell you why.

WHY YOUR BODY WAS MADE FOR RAW FOOD

To come to terms with what your body likes to have put into it, you just need to catch up a bit with the signs that your body has been giving you for a long time and understand that what you eat *does* affect how your body looks and feels. Unfortunately we often ignore these signs and just call them 'ageing', insisting that what we eat has nothing to do with how we look. If only this were true! When you *really* get your brain into gear it doesn't take long to realise that *everything* in your body is dependent on what you put in there – for better or worse. We are what we eat! Even the neurotransmitters in your brain go up and down depending on your intake of certain nutrients.

What exactly happens when you eat cooked food? This means the 'normal' diet; whether healthy and wholefood or terrible and junky. Wholefood is better than junk but it's still cooked.

Ever wondered why your face doesn't look as smooth as the inside of your arm? Protection, that's why. Your face is exposed all the time, the inside of your arm is protected. It stays smooth and significantly younger-looking than your face all your life. RR shows you how to minimise and even reverse this difference but the fact remains that extremes of heat and cold don't produce softness and freshness. And because this is Radical Rejuvenation we have to consider what happens on the inside. And the first thing that we notice is that cooked food is often eaten *hot*. And some foods, such as ice cream, are eaten very *cold* indeed. These extreme temperatures damage the inside of your body just as surely as the weather damages the visible, unprotected parts of your body, such as your face. The enzymes in your stomach are destroyed by hot food and drink. You begin to be deficient in nutrients simply because you *no longer have the capacity to extract these nutrients from your digestive tract*. Sounds too simple?

In our affluent society there is widespread chronic disease. There is a near-epidemic of osteoporosis in a society which over-consumes calcium-rich foods, there is a B12 deficiency in elderly meat eaters, there is anaemia, fatigue. There is 'old age'. With age and with *prolonged ingestion* of enzyme-deficient and enzyme-destructive foods, eaten hot and some very cold, *absorption* of nutrients becomes a real problem. Deficiencies can manifest *even without* deficient diets. Calcium in the West comes mostly from cheese, milk, yogurt, sardines. In other words, animal products which have been subjected to high temperatures. Cutting down on such foods and not eating your food hot or cold is the first step towards a younger body. This way you will ensure efficient digestion and absorption (the most important process of all for your well-being) of all the nutrients you take in with your food.

Here are some images to encourage you: Dr Ingelfinger, who specialises in gastroenterology, states that partial or almost complete malabsorption is quite common, resulting in disorders which are clinically recognised as colic disease, coeliac sprue and non-tropical sprue. Normal mucosal lining when viewed under magnification is lined with millions of villi, which move like miniature tentacles and assist the movement of partially digested material as well as its absorption. In sprue, for example, the villi are gone. What you see instead is a sterile-looking surface which resembles tanned hide. This process is caused by hot and cold foods. Similar harmful changes occur in your throat and on your tongue and some researchers see in them the precursors of cancer.

I suggest also that, if you eat 'hot' spicy food, you use garlic, onion and chilli in moderation and always mix them well into your meal to ensure that they cannot 'burn'. I have personally suffered quite nasty ulcers and painful burn patches in my mouth and throat as a result of eating very hot garlic and onion before I realised that I had to be careful. If they can do that in the mouth, they aren't going to be very good in the stomach. Oil is a traditional balm to the hotness of onion and garlic, so eating these foods in an oily dressing, mixed with avocado or in a nut sauce are all good ways of obtaining the benefits while avoiding the possibility of damage.

So what about room-temperature cooked food? Is that any better than hot? Not much to be honest. Because *all* cooked food, hot, cold or neutral, produces digestive leucocytosis. This is a term which describes a pathological increase in white blood cells. It occurs every time you eat cooked food and it never occurs when you eat raw food. This means that your body reacts to cooked food exactly as it would to an infection or a toxin. That is, your body views cooked food as a danger and a pathogen. This research was conducted by Dr Paul Kouchakoff who found that, although all cooked foods produced leucocytosis, pressure-cooked foods produced even more and highly processed foods such as white sugar, ham, wine and vinegar produced the most severe leucocytosis. He was working in the first three decades of the twentieth century so he didn't have the opportunity to examine the effects of microwaved and irradiated food on the human immune system, but I think we can all guess what his findings might have been.

Interestingly, even boiled water produces leucocytosis, which means that herb teas are treated as cooked food by the body. I'd say, however, that they are fine to use, especially in the beginning stages of RR when so many changes are going on. Allow them to cool down before drinking, though. Alcohol has a more obvious effect on your youthfulness, and, of course, it would be beneficial if you could try and give it up altogether, NOW. But I realise that for most people this just isn't realistic, so I suggest cutting alcohol down to *conscious* consuming. Keep the quality very high and the quantity very low. I can't, however, say the same for sugar, cigarettes and coffee because there is only so much abuse your body can take. An occasional glass of wine, preferably soon to be replaced by carrot juice, is all the sinning you can allow yourself to have if you don't want to look your age for many years to come.

Dr Kouchakoff found that you can avoid leucocytosis if you start each meal with raw foods and if at least eighty per cent of your food is raw. Other ways of minimising the effects of 'cheating' are: to reduce the damage caused by caffeine-containing beverages such as coffee, tea, chocolate or Coke, double the B complex in your daily supplement programme for that day. This means at least 50 mg of the major Bs such as B6, B1, B2 and B3. Also make sure you have taken your evening primrose oil, vitamin C and magnesium on such days of indulgence.

Other disasters caused by cooking include the destruction of enzymes, minerals and vitamins. Overcooking produces indigestible food which leads to all sorts of problems, such as free radical formation, the blocking of basement membranes and poor absorption and availability of nutrients. Overall not a very pretty picture. Frying is the worst offender – in fact, any process which turns food brown produces carcinogenic compounds Dried milk is also a highly over-cooked product and should be avoided, as should UHT milk and cream. The best cooking methods are poaching, steaming and baking, as long as the food is covered with a sauce and not browned or baked dry. 1 don't *really* recommend stir fry, even in extra virgin olive oil, sesame oil, butter, lard or anything else. But, if you have to, use a little olive or sesame oil.

By the way it is actually very hard to really cheat at RR by committing any of the above offences because your body instantly punishes you and then looking in the mirror will punish you again, so don't be tempted and remember the real crime is to yourself and your wellbeing. Try and follow as many positive steps as you can and your body will show that, too – you will look younger and feel more vibrant and alive.

SPECIAL RAW FOODS

I'm a great believer in magic foods. Some of the best additions to your rejuvenation programme are, of course, herbs. But there are also foods which act in the most miraculous ways to increase health, youthfulness and longevity if added regularly to your diet. Raw foods of all kinds have remarkable rejuvenating properties. Many researchers have contributed to our knowledge of raw food, among them Leslie Kenton, who has written very informative and intelligent books on the subject, Viktoras Kulvinskas, Ann Wigmore, Dr Max Bircher-Benner and Edmund Szekely.

Firstly raw foods are full of enzymes and secondly they give you vitality. All types of processing destroy this vitality including freezing, pasteurisation, smoking, pickling, pesticides, antibiotics (used by farmers quite regularly so try to use organic varieties). Air and water pollution also destroys much of value. *But* to get this into perspective: if you eat a *lot* of your food raw, and always a little at the start of every cooked meal, you will be going a long way towards looking and feeling better inside and out. Raw foods contain a whole universe of factors, many as yet undiscovered, many unobtainable in active supplemental form, which will protect you against old age.

PR IN ACTION

This is a case which illustrates the power of raw foods. Again, the subjects are animals, highlighting the fact that the effects of this approach, the raw food diet, are not 'all in the mind'. A cat was fed exclusively on good quality raw mince throughout her pregnancy and produced, with great ease, a litter of four, large, beautiful and healthy kittens. When these kittens had to be sold at eight weeks, the pet shop owner remarked on their obvious, robust health. One of these kittens was kept by the family who still owned the original queen. When this younger cat, the daughter, became pregnant, she was fed on standard tinned food because the raw diet became too expensive for two cats. This 'daughter', after a very difficult labour, produced three dead kittens which were completely undeveloped, one very small kitten which was very weak and one equally tiny kitten which became stuck in the cat's vagina and died. This very sad story echoes the findings of Dr Francis M. Pottenger who found very similar results when cats were fed cooked milk and meat, while cats fed on raw meat and raw milk thrived and were very lively and healthy.

Here are my favourite strongly rejuvenative foods.

Seaweed

Seaweed isn't really news to the beauty industry but it's effective as a beauty aid none the less. Seaweed produces seventy per cent of the earth's oxygen and, no matter where it originated, it will usually be pretty clean because seaweed has the ability to partially filter out and avoid absorbing much of the pollution from the water in which it grows. It also replaces itself very fast so that harvesting doesn't adversely affect its availability. It contains huge quantities of minerals – both essential and rare, all in forms highly assimilable by the body – as well as being high in protein.

Seaweed has the amazing ability to protect you against pollution, particularly radioactivity and heavy metals, helping your thyroid to function perfectly, improving the look of your skin and making your hair thicker. Kelp may at first seem difficult to love but you have to try because kelp will remove strontium-90, strontium-85, barium-140 and radium from your body. Besides, kelp powder actually tastes wonderful sprinkled on vegetables. Dulse will get rid of plutonium and the blue-green algae such as chlorella, spirulina and the algae from Lake Klamath will remove caesium-137. All seaweed contains sodium alginate which is responsible for some of this beneficial removal, but also the pigments of these (and other) plants contribute greatly to this effect. The colour of beetroot, for example, which is due to a bioflavonoid, also has pollution-protecting properties. There has been some suggestion that nori contains a B12 analogue – a form of B12 which may interfere with the function of B12 in the human body. However, a lot of evidence and human experience points to the possibility that people on raw, vegan diets make their own B12 – or, rather, that they have beneficial bacteria in the digestive tract which make this vitamin for them. Also, ironically, people who consume animal fats have a much higher requirement for this vitamin than people whose diets do not contain such fats.

Pollen

Pollen has been called the world's most perfect food. It is the pollen from flowers transformed by bees into a food with strongly rejuvenating qualities. Only about thirty per cent of pollen is collected by the beekeeper in specially designed traps placed at the entrance to a hive. It has been estimated that honeybee pollen contains over five thousand enzymes and co-enzymes. This, of course, is many times more than any other food.

Pollen protects against radiation, including X-rays and the radiotherapy used in cancer treatment, and can produce visible beneficial changes in the tone and pigmentation of ageing skin. Bee pollen also contains lecithin which protects the nervous system from ageing. Lecithin shields your body from the effects of many radioactive elements such as strontium-90, iodine-131, krypton-85, ruthenium-106, zinc-65, barium-140, potassium-42, caesium-137 and X-rays. Bee pollen also selectively protects the sex glands from radioactive iodine and plutonium. Some protection is also given against other environmental pollutants such as lead, mercury, aluminium, nitrites and nitrates, even DDT, which is still unfortunately present in our ecosystem. Pollen also contains nucleic acids which have been shown to be tremendously effective in halting and reversing the ageing process, tightening the skin and removing wrinkles, improving energy, vigour and vitality, particularly when taken regularly for a minimum of three months.

Pollen has also been found to increase life span. A group of mice, genetically bred to have a life span of only ten weeks, were given a diet of just pollen and distilled water and subsequently lived to be one and a half years old. Now that's quite an effect, isn't it!

A diet high in nucleic acids was first pioneered by Dr Benjamin Frank who had astonishing success with it, restoring elderly people to a youthful level of vitality and young-looking bodies. Dr

Frank advocated the use of sardines and brewer's yeast as nucleic acid sources, both of which I find difficult to recommend. I have tried the diet several times and brewer's yeast, in particular, is not a 'health' food I would recommend. It produces sluggishness, heaviness, painful joints or stiffness, which is a precursor to painful joints. Pollen provides all the nucleic acids and much more in a raw form, which is preferable.

In the opinion of Dr G. J. Binding, bee pollen is 'the finest food and best medicine ever discovered'. According to research in France, Russia and Italy, pollen is the richest source of protein in nature, containing five to seven times more protein than cheese, meat or eggs. It is also a valuable source of B12. It rejuvenates your whole glandular system and has strong anti-ageing properties. The best pollen is fresh and not processed in any way. Even people with hay fever and asthma have derived benefits from taking pollen, but begin slowly if you suffer from allergies. Start with just a few grains and increase slowly, monitoring reactions, and if you are at all worried, stop and seek the advice of a health professional. One to two teaspoons is a normal dose to provide you with tremendous anti-ageing power.

Honey

Beekeepers are the longest-living group of people in the world. As long as they eat honey, that is. However, when I say 'honey' I don't mean honey. Not the cooked, pasteurised, dead syrup from sugar-fed bees which is labelled, quite misleadingly in my opinion, 'honey' at your local supermarket. To get the real stuff you have to make friends with your local beekeeper or investigate your health food shop. Even there you have to exercise quite considerable caution; anything which is blended, a 'product of more than one country' and looks rather clear, uniform and 'polished' has been subjected to a lot of treatments to make it look pretty. Which means that most of its nutritional value has been poured down the drain somewhere. This is why I have often said that honey is too sweet and not suitable for the RR Diet. However, if you keep looking, you will find it. It will probably be a bit rougher looking than its pasteurised sisters but it will taste delicious and it will be good for you! Cold-processed honeys are making an entrance into our health food shops and about time, too!

Of course, this sort of honey that the long-living beekeepers eat is full of pollen, still contains some wax and possesses active enzymes. So you have to do a little 'doctoring' to your shop-bought jar. If you have a cold-processed product then the enzymes are still active. Add powdered pollen to your jar of honey and mix well in. That way you'll be getting a real dynamo of rejuvenation each time you dip into your jar. You can grind the pollen in a coffee grinder to obtain a powder. Or just make sure you take a spoonful of pollen each time you have some honey. For an even better energy boost, add some royal jelly (see the following section) and take propolis drops. Your energy will be better than you've known for years! Honey has been used for arthritis, insomnia, coughs and colds. Mick Jagger and other singers gargle with honey to keep their singing equipment in good working order. Honey helps your body retain calcium. *Raw* honey, that is. It's also interesting that raw honey does not hurt the teeth but processed honey produced by sugar-fed bees can hurt sensitive teeth quite a bit! This is another reason to find a good, unprocessed honey from wild bees, if possible. Many beekeepers feed the bees on white sugar in the winter. However, even though honey is undoubtedly delicious, I recommend that you use it sparingly because it's so very sweet.

Royal Jelly

Everybody knows this by now: the queen bee lives for years and is fed on royal jelly. Her workers, on the other hand, live just weeks and they eat no royal jelly. Pantothenic acid is a B vitamin found in large quantities in royal jelly. Its discoverer, Dr Roger Williams, considers it a very valuable substance in prolonging human life span. Of course, pantothenic acid is just one of many life-enhancing substances found in the remarkable life-giving complex we call royal jelly.

Queen bees are not born that way; they are made from ordinary bees and turn into queens when fed royal jelly. It is made from pollen and honey by nurse bees. These are just some of the amazing substances found in royal jelly: it is a rich source of natural hormones, contains an abundance of B vitamins, plus vitamins A, C and E; it contains twenty amino acids, including cystine; it is a very rich source of DNA and RNA, both of which are highly effective rejuvenators; it also contains a precursor of collagen, a powerful anti-ager. Finally, royal jelly enhances immune function and has a powerful antibiotic effect.

Royal jelly has long been considered to be a life-prolonging and regenerating substance. It increases your sex drive and makes you look and feel years younger. So what are you waiting for? Go get some!

Propolis

This is the substance which bees make from tree resin to protect their hives. Not only has propolis been found to protect people against colds, coughs and mouth ulcers, it has been used to regenerate bone. Use it in tincture form in conjunction with all the other honey products (you can even chew a piece of beeswax to complete your 'Bee Program' – it has also been shown to have beneficial properties). Tincture is the easiest way to use it because in its solid form propolis is very chewy indeed! Propolis has sometimes been found to be high in lead if the trees which the bees collect the sap from are near a busy road, so buy from a reputable company which tests for lead content.

Of course, bee products are made by 'animals', but they are, literally, light years away from the animal proteins I have been cautioning you about. As you will find out when you use them. In fact, I'll let you in on a BIG secret – even if you do not alter your diet one bit, as long as you begin to use bee products every day, you will experience quite amazing levels of health and rejuvenation!

I recommend all bee products from the CC Pollen Company

(see Sources at the back of the book). Also the Herbal Apothecary will supply you with high-quality bee products.

Avocado

This is my favourite raw food. Avocado makes a very good substitute for meat with no harmful effects whatsoever. It contains protein, minerals, vitamins and EFAs, all in easily assimilated form. Don't worry about calories either. On a raw diet you discover your best body. Just remember what every farmer knows – pigs fed on cooked potatoes put on weight like a dream. Pigs fed raw potatoes stay thin and good looking!

One of the most intriguing findings about the avocado is that it contains a factor which stimulates the growth of young, fresh skin. It works both internally and on external application. It is extremely rich in vitamin E, vitamin C and beta carotene, all of which are free radical scavengers and essential for youthful looks. It also contains folic acid and other B vitamins and is extremely good food for those recovering from illness. It is even suggested that avocado can increase sexual vigour! So go for the green one and spice up your life and your sex drive.

Beetroot

Even if you don't have Slavic ancestors you ought to get into beetroot. It is high in iron and very effective in treating anaemia. It will also protect your body against radioactive forms of iron, plutonium and caesium. It can reverse and prevent the formation of radiation-induced cancers and can also offer protection against leukaemia. The anti-cancer compounds are closely bound to the colouring matter of beetroots. As you know, oxygen is vital to youthful cell function and beetroot has a strong ability to increase cellular uptake of oxygen. To obtain the benefits from this vegetable you have to eat it in its raw state, either as fresh juice (mixed with carrot juice for a delicious youth-booster drink) or blended with carrots, various fresh fruits and dried sultanas (always use organic dried fruits wherever possible),

Gou Qi Zi berries and water as a sort of a health cocktail for breakfast, lunch or supper. Or you could simply grate or chop it into your salads.

Carrots

A single carrot contains seven different, active anti-cancer compounds. It also contains enough beta carotene to give you the basic recommended dose for one day, is a fantastic liver tonic and protects your lungs against cancer. Carrots will also protect you from the damaging effects of ultraviolet radiation from inside out and, externally in the form of carrot oil, will greatly minimise the formation of sun-induced wrinkles. Carrots are also very good for your coronary arteries and as free radical scavengers.

Shii-ta-ke Mushrooms

The average person takes two *kilograms* of chemical additives into their body every year. FRIGHTENING! Fortunately there are ways of helping your body to cope with modern life other than emigrating to a distant planet. Recently a whole group of medicinally active plants have come to the attention of Western doctors, researchers and lay people because of their powerful immuno-stimulatory properties. These are mushrooms. Not the button mushrooms we're used to but their oriental cousins, particularly the shii-ta-ke (*Lentinus edodes*) and the reishi (called Ling Zhi in Chinese and *Ganoderma lucidum* in Latin). Reishi has been used with great success in cancer therapy, in the treatment of allergies and against pollution damage. It was renowned by the Chinese Taoist masters as an immortality elixir when extracted in alcohol, which is its most potent form. Shii-ta-ke mushrooms have recently begun appearing in the supermarkets next to their cousins the button mushrooms. You can use them raw in salads, unlike the reishi mushroom, which is hard and inedible in its dry form. Even dry shii-ta-ke can be used – simply soak for an hour or so in some water, cut and add to your salads. Lentinan, derived from the shii-ta-ke, is now recognised as the most powerful natural immune stimulant known. It restores T-lymphocyte function in cancer patients and increases the production of interferon. In Japan it is now routinely used in the treatment of stomach and colon cancers.

Spirulina

Once, when I offered my two-and-a-half-year-old son some spirulina in water he informed me that he preferred plasticine. So much for the taste! Do try it, though. It isn't that bad. In fact I like it and the results are much more spectacular than if you'd been indulging in plasticine.

There are many blue-green algae available: spirulina, chlorella, the algae from Lake Klamath and Phyto Plankton made by BioCare. Vitamin B12, which is found in all the blue-green algae, may be in the form of a B12 analogue, particularly in chlorella and spirulina. This analogue possibly makes B12 unavailable to the human body because it may interfere with human-active B12. There is no definitive evidence on this question yet, but I would recommend a good vitamin supplement anyway, one which contains vitamin B12 but which does *not* contain iron or copper. Or take VitaSorb B12 made by BioCare. Take it separately from your spirulina or other blue-green algae, preferably with a twelve-hour gap between the two. Or use blue-green algae from Lake Klamath which is very high in human-active B12 and has not been found to contain B12 analogues. New evidence from research carried out by Dr Gabriel Cousens has shown that both spirulina and Lake Klamath algae contain human-active B12.

The reason why I trust spirulina is that it is a living complex and many times during the modern investigation of herbs so-called toxins and harmful effects were found which did indeed produce undesirable effects *when isolated from the parent plant* by artificial and chemical procedures. When taken as the whole plant, however, no such effects were observed. It is therefore important to realise that many of the recent scares about herbs have been the result of such scientifically stilted investigation which pays no heed to the harmony, synergy and complexity of plant forms. Plus, the study which brought the question of B12 analogues into prominence was not at all conclusive in the case of spirulina. If anything, it seemed to provide evidence against macrobiotic diets for children and possibly that nori is a source of B12 analogues. Even this, however, was not really rock-solid science.

Spirulina contains EFAs of the Omega 3 and Omega 6 groups and also a good amount of gamma linolenic acid (GLA). It is a source of complete protein, one of the richest sources of beta carotene, contains vitamin E, the B complex, calcium, iron, zinc, manganese, magnesium, chromium and selenium. It is also a rich source of enzymes if it has been carefully dried. It protects the body against the damaging effects of pollution and detoxifies it from heavy metals. It is a rich source of the plant pigment chlorophyll, which gives leaves their green colour. Chlorophyll acts in the human body much as your own haemoglobin would, increasing energy and helping the oxygenation of tissues. Other plant pigments, such as the red colour in beetroots and the carotenoids in carrots, have excellent cancer-protecting properties.

Garlic

Garlic has to be raw and strong smelling, otherwise its good effects are destroyed. Garlic oil capsules are pretty much useless. I know that lots of good research has been done on Kyolic, so if you really can't bear the thought of the real thing opt for Kyolic. *But* I still prefer the real raw garlic clove to any other preparation. Always mix it with other veggies, preferably something smooth and soothing such as an avocado, or make it into a dressing with walnut, hazelnut or linseed oil to avoid burning your mouth, tongue and the rest of your digestive tract.

Garlic will protect you against a whole host of Dracula-like nasties – botulism, tuberculosis, dysentery, staphylococcus infections and typhoid fever. This wonderful, tasty plant is the broadest spectrum antibiotic around. It has antibacterial, antifungal, antiparasitic, antiprotozoan and antiviral effects. And allicin, the smelly compound in garlic, is mostly responsible for these actions. This is why in my opinion deodorised garlic is not as good as raw, fresh garlic. However, I must add that Japanese Kyolic garlic extracts have performed very well in studies and seem to be very similar in their action to that of raw garlic. So you do have a choice.

Garlic fights influenza, colds, candida, whooping cough, cryptococcal meningitis, pneumonia and intestinal infections. However the most interesting thing about garlic is that it augments immune function. If you eat garlic your natural killer cells will be 140 to 160 per cent more effective in destroying cancer cells. And just two cloves of garlic per day will protect you from colds. Some researchers also believe that garlic will offer help in AIDS by revving up the immune system and protecting the patient against the many opportunistic infections which afflict AIDS sufferers. Good immune function is essential to longevity and youthfulness. In fact, garlic was one of the herbs used to significantly increase life span by the Chinese. The other herbs were He Shou Wu, ginseng and Gotu Kola.

Garlic is excellent for the heart, lowering the harmful LDL blood cholesterol and triglycerides and raising the levels of beneficial HDL cholesterol. Low doses of garlic can even mend vulnerable arteries. Five cloves daily are sufficient for clinical effects, while two cloves a day make a good protection programme.

Garlic has also proved to be a star in the treatment of thrombosis due to a recently discovered component called ajoene. This garlic compound has been found to be as effective as aspirin without any side-effects. Again, my recommendation is to use the whole, raw food. Who knows what other magical compounds are still waiting to be discovered? Eat garlic and have the lot!

Perhaps the most exciting property of garlic is the one most relevant to rejuvenation. Garlic has been found to be even better than vitamin E as an anti-oxidant. It will prevent all sorts of cancers and, since it has a special affinity for the lungs, should be a regular part of your rejuvenation programme if you have been or still are a smoker.

Onion

The benefits for garlic and onion are very similar. I suggest you eat both daily and get even more adventurous by adding red onions to your diet whenever you can. Red onion is very high in quercetin, another high-power bioflavonoid which has strong anti-cancer and anti-pollution activity.

Lemon

Apart from protecting you against scurvy, lemon peel has remarkably powerful anti-oxidant properties which, of course, make it a major contender against cancer and ageing. We always add one whole lemon to our daily 'mix' which is a delicious blend of fruit, beetroot and carrots and makes a nourishing meal or snack. Lemons are, of course, spectacularly rich in vitamin C and the bioflavonoids. They also contain B vitamins. Lemon is wonderful at stopping colds and extremely valuable in the treatment of respiratory diseases. The peel contains potent bactericides, is a great liver tonic and activates the immune system.

Bilberries, Blackberries and Other Berries

When I was a young child in Czechoslovakia one of our closest friends was Dr Stanislav Novak, who had once been involved in cancer research. He told us that he had been very close to finding what he saw as a cure for cancer but that at that point the authorities intervened, shut down his laboratory and he ended up in prison where he remained for sixteen years. He said he could no longer remember the complete findings of his work because there had been some attempts at brainwashing in the prison. All he could remember was that he had found a biologically active, important anti-cancer factor in berries. It pleases me very much, therefore, when I read that 'new' research all over the world is pointing to bioflavonoids as being perhaps the most potent anti-cancer and anti-ageing compounds. Bioflavonoids are found in very high concentrations in all sorts of berries and you should eat them often. Bilberries are, in addition, excellent for varicose veins and can be used with absolute safety in pregnancy, a time when this problem often appears for the first time or becomes much more serious and when, of course, drugs are not desirable.

Sprouted Nuts, Seeds, Grains and Pulses

These are growing foods and for rejuvenation that's good news. They are filled with enzymes and growing factors and will help you look your best. Use them every single day. As soon as a seed, grain or pulse is moistened, remarkable changes begin. Vitamins, minerals, amino acids and enzymes reach extraordinarily high levels during sprouting. Starch is turned into easily assimilable carbohydrate, fat into fatty acids, protein into amino acids. Sprouts even contain vitamin B12. But the most exciting finding is that sprouts can, literally, make you grow younger.

When old, decrepit rats, whose age corresponded to a human age of ninety, were placed on a diet of immature foods such as sprouts and still-growing leaves which had not yet finished their complete cycle, the old rats were transformed; their bodies began to grow young again. One of the factors responsible for this effect is anxinon, an enzyme found in the growing portion of a young shoot. Dr Ann Wigmore and Viktoras Kulvinskas use immature plants and raw food to reverse the progress of many varied conditions such as emphysema, grey hair, even leukaemia and Parkinson's disease. Such a diverse range of therapeutic effects can only be explicable in terms of a strong rejuvenating, revitalising and re-balancing effect of the immature plants. Sprouts are also incredibly high in nucleic acids. And, of course, the synergy of these factors means that taken as a whole, in the living, sprouting plant, you are getting a veritable anti-ageing dynamo! A word about seeds and nuts. Most of these have been treated and so they are not really raw. The notable exceptions are almonds, alfalfa, fenugreek and sunflower seeds. All of these will sprout when soaked, can be eaten after twelve hours in water and are real superfoods. All other nuts and seeds are inferior, even when soaked. Cashew nuts are perhaps the worst. However, when you are in transition use whatever you fancy to help you into a more raw and healthy way of eating. For this reason you will find recipes featuring all sorts of nuts, even cashews, in the recipe section. You can always cut them out and replace them with almonds later.

Herbs and Spices

I can't live without these! They have been used to maintain the health of people all over the world for centuries and with good reason; herbs such as thyme, oregano and rosemary are extremely potent anti-oxidants, turmeric has strong liver-protecting activity, chilli and cayenne stimulate the immune system. So make friends with the herbs and spices! Eat them raw and eat them often.

CHANGING HABITS

What Can You Use to Wash Your Hair and Face?

As far as I am concerned, the best shampoo and face wash must be *edible*. Bio-degradable is better than what we used to use, but let's face it, if you had a goldfish, you wouldn't feed it bio-degradable washing-up liquid. And your skin absorbs almost anything you put on it. So your shampoo and face wash ought to be something you wouldn't mind finding in your tooth mug if you were brushing your teeth in the river. Even Helena Rubinstein is reputed to have said that you should never put anything on your face that you wouldn't put in your mouth. Here are some ideas for cleansing products which are not only harmless but positively good for you and the environment:

Instead of soap and water or a commercial cleanser wet your face, apply a layer of extra virgin olive oil, then pour some Celtic sea salt in the palm of your hand and massage all over your face (including neck), then rinse with warm water. This will effectively remove make-up and dead cells, giving you a wonderful exfoliating treatment which will leave your skin looking pink, glowing and smooth. To remove mascara moisten some cotton wool with walnut oil and carefully and gently wipe over your eyelashes. Keep your eyes closed and remove excess oil with a soft towel.

Moistened fine oatmeal makes a good face wash. You can use ground almonds instead, or powdered marshmallow root. Or you can soak some linseed overnight in water and in the morning whizz it up in the blender and wash your face with the gel. It will wash and soften your skin beautifully.

For your hair mix some marshmallow root powder with some water to make a slightly runny paste and use as you would any shampoo. Rinse well. If you have blonde or dark blonde hair add camomile powder to the basic marshmallow shampoo but be careful if your hair has been in any way colour-treated or permed; in that case do a strand test to be safe. Add some lemon juice to increase the lightening effects. For dark hair which has not been treated with chemicals or dyes (even natural) add sage powder to the marshmallow. These are true herb shampoos, with the medicinal properties completely intact; detergents destroy the activity of herbs and commercial 'herb' products are often completely inactive. This shampoo will really look after your hair and it smells really wonderful, unlike many of the 'herb' shampoos you find in shops. Rinse the shampoo well with clear water.

You can make another good shampoo by simply boiling a sliced lemon or two in water until the peel has gone very soft. Blend it and you have a wonderful cleansing treatment which really brightens dull hair.

Fuller's earth, kaolin or bentonite powder can be mixed to a paste with some water in the blender and then used as a shampoo. Rinse very well with lots of clear water. If you find it too drying, add a teaspoon of glycerine (vegetable glycerine preferably) to the shampoo. Add a little organic apple cider vinegar to the last rinsing water or apply it to your hair and then rinse.

These natural shampoos need a little more 'elbow grease' when you are working them through your hair and you need to wash them out very thoroughly. But they produce lovely results, are completely harmless and are also very cheap. The best conditioner is coconut, walnut or sesame oil, applied before you shampoo your hair. Use several washes so that you are left with clean, shiny, young-looking hair.

The RR Make-over

When you start the RR programme you will probably find that you no longer have to use make-up because you will have no wrinkles to hide, spots to cover up or uneven skin patches to smother beneath layers of foundation which starve the skin and block pores. Your bare face will be glowing and beautiful without touching it up. You can wave goodbye to those expensive preparations too. Your eyes will be naturally shiny and lashes long and healthy. Your lips, uncracked and really kissable. Cheeks glowing naturally – no need for streaks of blusher. The money you save can be spent on RR supplements, essential oils, herbs, minerals, vitamins – a much more worthwhile and long lasting cause.

A New Treat for Teeth

We all tend to think that our dental health actually depends on foam and detergent. In my experience, however, toothpaste often does very little *except* foam. You can make a really simple and effective toothpowder which leaves your teeth feeling clean and looking shiny *and* doesn't even cost a lot. Take equal parts of Celtic sea salt and powdered or just dried sage. Mix very well and run through a grinder. Keep in an airtight container in the bathroom. That's it. When you want to use it, dampen your toothbrush, dip into the mixture and gently but thoroughly clean your teeth. Rinse well to make sure you remove any particles of sage that may be lodged between your teeth and don't worry about the salt in this toothpaste – you rinse most of it out.

Another good toothpowder is made from bicarbonate of soda and sea salt, mixed together in a proportion of 2:1. It gently removes stains and polishes your teeth to shiny smoothness. A toothpaste based on this recipe has hooked about 20 million Americans. Use this cheap, simple and effective preparation and find out why. To make it even nicer, add two or three drops of essential peppermint oil.

Liquorice powder (either Chinese or Western) is a superb tooth powder. It heals mouth ulcers *instantly* and prevents tooth decay.

If you have gum problems, use pure cayenne powder. Yes, it's hot, but not too bad. Brush your teeth and your gums. Some people have avoided gum surgery with this simple treatment alone. Cayenne is also very effective at stopping tooth and gum pain and mouth pain after chemotherapy.

A Cleansing Tonic as You Change to RR

As you start to change your diet and move to the RR way you may experience nausea or headaches as the toxins that have been trapped inside your body for years work their way out. You can minimise the discomfort by simply stirring one teaspoon of bentonite clay powder or pectin powder into a mug of distilled, spring or filtered water and drinking it down. This is a very effective, instant remedy for removing toxins out of the body and you should feel better almost immediately. Repeat as necessary.

Painful Periods

You don't have to have painful periods, heavy bleeding or dark clotted blood. The worst PMT, painful periods and related discomforts such as painful varicose veins that I have ever experienced was when I added meat to my diet, even though it was organic and free range. I also found that wheat and barley, dairy products, margarine and even excessive vegetable fats led to painful periods. To begin with, try cutting out all animal products five days before your period is due. Eat baked potatoes instead of wheat products and add plenty of fresh fruit and veg to your diet.

Foods Which Are Not Recommended on the RR Programme

Most of these RR no-nos are obvious but it is best to get them clear in your mind before you start. They are:

    white sugar
    white flour products
    white rice

red meat
saturated fat
alcohol
coffee
tea
smoked and pickled foods

When you eat a better diet you become a better person. For example the diet of prisoners was vastly improved when sugar, together with refined flour products, was replaced with fresh fruit, wholemeal flour and generally more wholesome foods. Their behaviour improved dramatically. There were fewer fights and arguments and their overall attitude was far more positive and constructive. Having taught nutrition in a prison I can assure you that the food in these institutions is appallingly bad. In fact prison is one of the places where one can still find clinical vitamin deficiencies in the West. Hospitals are another.

CUTTING OUT SUGAR

Concentrated sugar in all its forms is responsible for mood swings, lowered immunity and pre-diabetic conditions, to name but a few. So what do you do about the craving for sweetness? This craving is actually good for you. It helped you to survive as a baby – mother's milk is incredibly sweet and babies love it. The answer to this craving is simple – fresh fruit. We live in a privileged society so you can have fresh fruit all year round and satisfy your craving healthily and in a way that makes you look and feel better and younger. However, even fresh fruit can cause tooth deterioration because of acidity, so RR includes supplements to protect you against these possible effects: silica, magnesium and calcium.

If you really can't give up all that sweetness in one go then I suggest you throw out everything apart from a small jar of pure, *raw* organic honey. This is a valuable food. Though, for the sake of your teeth, brush well with cayenne and liquorice powder after eating anything sweet. Dried fruit, although not strictly 'raw' in the live sense of that word (non-organic fruit, even 'sun-dried', is oven-dried after washing and organic dried fruit is deep frozen, too, to kill bacteria), can still be a valuable part of your RR diet. Eat it with grains, in mixes, make 'sweeties', sweet sauces, pie crusts. You can eat it soaked or straight from the packet, but remember your teeth. And never eat the sulphured varieties, such as the bright orange apricots, peaches, papaya and pears.

STOPPING SALT

Salt is perhaps easier to give up than sugar but if you find it difficult here is a way to do it, step by step:

Step One

Substitute Celtic sea salt for your usual salt, even if you are using sea salt already. Celtic salt is harvested gently by hand rather than by bulldozer and does not require extensive washing which leads to a loss of minerals. This superb salt also contains good quantities of magnesium. However look out for those bags under your eyes first thing in the morning – it means your kidneys are being overworked which means that if you are using salt you ought to cut it out or, at the very least, cut down.

Step Two

Cut down. Use salt less often or use less of it. Start adding herbs, including black pepper, which has a nice, strong taste and does seem to provide the same sort of tastebud stimulation that salt gives. Kelp powder or dulse flakes are also good salt substitutes, and full of minerals. Kelp is better because it is not as salty as dulse. Try eating foods without flavourings. Have you ever had fresh raw corn on the cob? Mmmmm!

Step Three

Cut it out. You'll know when you have reached this stage because you won't actually miss the salt at all. If it takes you a year that's fine.

BYE-BYE TO HANGOVERS AND OTHER ALCOHOL NASTIES

With the alcohol the straight answer is of course, DON'T. But that's not so easy to do for most people and of course there are social occasions when you wish to indulge, so cut down to the occasional drink. There are plenty of designer non-alcoholic drinks so try to get into them when you go out or are at a party where it is difficult not to drink. Try and buy organic wine if you can. Eat black grapes – they will give you the beneficial bioflavonoids which are in reality responsible for most of the beneficial effects of wine. And if you absolutely have to have a drink, enjoy it and take plenty of vitamin B complex and evening primrose oil both before and after your drinking session to minimise the bad effects of alcohol.

Health Warning – Smoking

Smoking is extremely good for making wrinkles and not all that good for the rest of you. One cigarette destroys 25 mg of vitamin C in your body, so take this vitamin regularly if you smoke. 500 mg a day should do it. Also take vitamin E and eat lots of carrots or drink carrot juice. Carrots have been shown to protect the lungs of smokers against lung cancer. Garlic, almonds and sprouts such as mung beans will also keep your lungs in the best working order possible.

Don't forget that if you live with or work with a smoker you need to protect your body just as much as a smoker does. So take the supplements described above.

Get into Salads and Other Raw Goodies

Begin to add more frequent and bigger salads to your meals, sometimes replacing and other times *almost* elbowing out the cooked component. Have a raw breakfast or lunch, aim for raw days. This can take years. Take your time. Put sunlight on your plate and get into the colour of raw foods. Cooked foods have to be artificially coloured to have eye-appeal. But the natural colours in raw food are really beautiful, as you will be when you eat them. Fall in love with those beautiful shades of red and orange in red peppers and carrots, the purple of red cabbage, the exquisite hue of ripe mango and papaya, the richness of sharon fruit, the pretty green of limes – suddenly food becomes an art form instead of a charred and greasy mess. Use all the colours which nature has provided and you will receive all the nutrients you need to grow younger and healthier. These colours, by the way, are health-giving pigments which protect you against ageing, pollution and many diseases.

Revolutionise Your Kitchen

Out with the microwave, the cooker, the grill, the oven, the toaster, the freezer and in with juicers and blenders. These are the only pieces of specialised equipment necessary for RR (except a good fridge of course). Buy a large blender/grinder with an easily washable, sturdy jug. Most shops which sell kitchen equipment will have something to suit your taste and purse. Buy the largest jug you can, to accommodate large quantities of blended foods. Most juicers are centrifugal and this is perfect for all the juicing suggested in this book. Much less washing-up too. No more grimy cooker cleaning and grill scraping.

WHAT ABOUT EXERCISE?

If you need to do 200 sit-ups to get a flat tummy, you're eating the wrong foods. But the benefits of exercise are so numerous that it is an absolute must for RR, especially if you are still eating some cooked food. As you increase the percentage of raw food in your diet you will notice that your body is stronger and more supple between exercise sessions and remains in condition for longer even if you miss your normal workouts. Paradoxically, even though you actually need to do it less, you will enjoy exercise so much that you will do it more and it will be more fun, too.

I suggest that you do a workout that combines yoga and aerobics so that you get the best of both worlds. Yoga is unequalled in promoting superb bodily function and aerobics add to it by building a good-looking outline, releasing endorphins which make you smile for the rest of the day, increasing your basal metabolic rate which means that your body is burning calories even as you *sleep*, releasing wonderful, rejuvenating growth hormone, improving circulation and making you feel more sexy! Aerobic exercise also increases bone density, and so prevents osteoporosis, and strengthens your heart. Yoga will protect you against stiff joints, arthritis, high blood pressure and varicose veins; the upside-down postures are great fun for helping your hair and making your face more youthful as well as improving brain function.

To really benefit from your exercise routine you ought to do it every day. But even I don't, so go for four days a week, twenty minutes each of yoga and an aerobic routine. I find the best way to do aerobics is on a mini-trampoline – I 'run' so that I am comfortably out of breath which is the best way to get muscle-sculpting benefits.

The best way to do yoga is to perform the postures which you really like and do them slowly and gently. Never strain. The very best yoga book is the one you like and use! It is, of course, a good idea to work on your whole body at every session and to balance the stretches so that you bend both ways.

If yoga and aerobics don't appeal you could always try a martial art. The best ones combine stretching with speed and will build up your self-confidence, too. You could try aikido or wushu, for instance. My family is full of martial artists, from the tiniest two-year-old who has developed the most wonderful 'centred' stance, to Daddy who teaches aikido; in between is a four-year-old who has a go at everything and attempts to throw everyone and a ten-year-old daughter who looks very beautiful when doing her wushu forms. I used to do aikido as often as I could before I had my last two babies. Personally I am attracted to the dynamic yet beautiful arts such as aikido and wushu but if you feel that you'd like to try something different, such as tai chi or judo, then go ahead and find a good class. In my experience, nothing compares with the glow, self-confidence and sheer attitude you get from martial arts practice.

I have found that the worse the diet is, the more exercise you have to do, and the better your diet, the more you can do. Together a great diet and an energetic lifestyle are a dynamite combination. You wake up *and* go to bed smiling!

A word about sunshine. I know that to prevent wrinkles we are supposed to wear a sunscreen all year, every day. But you will find that, as you cut out sugar, alcohol and salt and increase raw foods which are rich in protective factors, your skin will be far less affected by the sun. I don't think we should get too hysterical about this whole thing: sunshine is wonderful. Besides, you *need* it to make vitamin D. I think the best way to treat your skin in the sun is to wear a mild sunscreen (such as the one I described in the chapter on skin) and protect your skin with VitaSorb C (or vitamin C powder dissolved in water); VitaSorb E (or another product containing pure vitamin E) and a cream which contains propolis. Propolis is a bee product – bees use it to protect their hives from infection. It protects us, too, and has been found to repair and prevent sun damage.

Your body is a dynamic, complex system. It functions with precision and intelligence *if* allowed to do so. As you begin to follow the principles of RR you will become more alert and more vibrant and you will enjoy foods which support you in feeling that way. A positive spiral comes into being and you start to enjoy your life and the way you look more than you've ever done before. Bye-bye stressed out and getting old and hello to calm, relaxed, young and confident. You will find that other areas of your life – your relationships with others, work, family and studies – will all start to work well as you start to feel better about yourself. Far from being tied down by this new way of eating, you end up having liberated yourself and having an extraordinary amount of energy for the sheer enjoyment of your life. Remember even just a raw carrot before each meal is a start. So get going and get looking not just good but great!

CHAPTER ELEVEN

Radical Rejuvenation Food and Recipes

I love reading recipes, but I've never actually followed one. It was the same when I was trying to be a scientist – I always managed to change a little something at least once, even in biochemistry. Cookery's more fun in that respect – change can bring improvement. However, even though I seem to be completely unable to follow instructions, I love giving them! So in this chapter you will find them; lots of instructions, hints, recipes and ideas. I hope you'll find yourself unable to follow them at least some of the time and that you will discover for yourself the pleasure of using raw ingredients creatively and elegantly. Everything from simple, quick snacks to picnics and buffets and parties is possible without even a hint of a look in your cooker's direction. The real plus about eating raw foods is that they are quick, simple, fresh and good for you. No more slaving in a hot, steamy kitchen either. And the results, as I'm sure you'll discover, surpass all expectations with regard to taste and eye appeal. Even smell! Our house smells wonderful even though we hardly ever even boil water for herb tea. So now let's get familiar with the raw ingredients.

NUTS AND SEEDS

As I have said already in the chapter on enzymes, I don't recommend the frequent use of unsoaked nuts or seeds because they contain enzyme inhibitors. However, cashew nuts and almonds in moderation can be useful for filling out and giving body to vegetable loaves and used with discretion I have found no problems with them. But if you find they leave you unpleasantly full or bloated, substitute soaked, well-drained sunflower seeds. Nuts such as brazils, almonds and hazelnuts are delicious soaked. Give them a full twenty-four hours in clean water and you'll be astonished – instead of a heavy, fattening nut you have something light and fresh, something closer to a vegetable than a nut. You can leave them for three or four days and they'll just keep getting better. Change the water and rinse the nuts every twelve hours. Almonds are easy to peel after soaking and you'll actually see them begin to sprout. Sunflower seeds make wonderful sprouts; just cover them in clean water and four to six hours later you have a bowlful of tasty and very nutritious snacks/salad fillers/stuffing for nori rolls/thickener for smoothies when blended with bananas.

Soaking not only gets rid of the unwelcome enzyme inhibitors which get washed away in the soaking water (so don't use this liquid, with the exception of the water from soaking wheat berries. This is called rejuvelac and many people find it a very beneficial, healing drink. Use it by all means if it agrees with you. You will find instructions for making rejuvelac in the section on grains in this chapter), it also breaks down or 'pre-digests' the protein in the nuts and seeds which means that the amino acids can be quickly utilised for repair and building of healthy tissue. In fact, the most times I've ever been asked for my 'beauty secret' was when I was virtually living on sprouts (and an all-raw diet, of course). Lentil and sunflower, if you want to know. I find it wonderful that in a world where a pot of beauty cream can cost as much as one family's weekly food bill the real secrets are still contained in something as unassuming as a little green sprouted seed.

Soaked linseed is useful as a thickener for sauces and dressings. Blend very well with fresh water before using. It's a very useful source of the important Omega 3 fatty acids. Cashew nuts are a bit of a 'problem soaker' – they become slimy and mouldy very quickly, in a matter of hours, and I think they are better left out of the water altogether. Pine kernels, on the other hand, almost blossom in water, so do try them. As with all seeds, four to eight hours are sufficient to remove most of the enzyme inhibitors but you can continue for up to twenty-four hours. Sunflower seeds are fine soaked for several days, provided you keep them well covered with water and change it every twelve hours. Buckwheat (which is a seed, not a grain) doesn't seem to do anything except sit there and go mouldy, but do try it – you may have a better batch or better luck than me. Sesame and pumpkin seeds develop a yummy crunchiness when soaked. Don't soak any seeds from the nightshade family such as tomato or potato as they are poisonous. Also keep away from red kidney beans in raw form – they are very poisonous. Fava beans (even when cooked) can cause poisoning in susceptible people.

Remember that shelled nuts and seeds sold in shops are often *not* raw; many undergo heat and other treatments during the shelling process. However, when you are in the transition stage between cooked food and raw you can use shelled nuts and seeds if they agree with you. Do try and use those which are raw as much as possible. These are: almonds, sunflower seeds, alfafa seeds, and linseed (known as flax seed in America).

GRAINS AND PULSES

Yes, they can be eaten raw as long as you sprout them. Some people use soaked grain flakes (which are actually steam-processed) and flour, but I find them heavy and very mucus forming. A quick way to a blocked nose. So I stay away. Although ground whole oat groats make a good raw porridge, especially when sweetened with chunks of dates or raisins. And I love sprouted wheat. Wheat is something which used to cause me great problems in its cooked form but I can eat it in its sprouted form quite freely. And many other people find this to be true for them, too. It's one of the magic qualities of raw foods. And, of course, raw wheat is a thousand times better for you than cooked. Wheat sprouts are delicious as a filling for a nori roll. The only thing that can improve the taste is a little finely chopped garlic together with 'Yummy Green Sauce' which you will find on page 201.

All grains and pulses take far longer to sprout and become digestible than do seeds and nuts. The longest sprouters, such as soya bean and chickpea, need at least two days of soaking before you can use them. I'd leave them at least two days after this time to grow a bit, too. They develop a succulent freshness at this stage and are much easier on your digestion. Change the soaking water every twelve hours and rinse the beans well each time. Lentils (brown and green, not red. The red ones are split and will not sprout as well as the whole ones, although, surprisingly, some of them do sprout), mung beans and wheat are easy; leave them well covered in water overnight – the pulses, especially, swell considerably during soaking time. Give them lots of room and water. Rinse in the morning and leave them to grow. Rinse at least twice each day. Eat when the small, white shoots begin to grow. You may wish to let green lentils and mung beans grow for a longer time, in which case they become much lighter and more like a vegetable than a pulse. If the lentils begin to grow green leaves they are still fine to eat and very delicious, too. But don't let wheat shoots become too long – they are tough.

If you would like to try rejuvelac, which can be used as a starter for fermented products such as cheeses and yogurt (more about these delicious treats later on in this chapter), simply let the wheat berries stand covered with water for twenty-four hours. Strain and keep the liquid. This is rejuvelac. You may drink it as it is or use it for making cheese or yogurt. It will keep for a day in the fridge. One batch of wheat berries will yield three lots of rejuvelac over as many days. It is a highly regarded vitality supplement, so do try it. It should taste lovely – if it is sour or unpleasant then it's off. Throw it out and start again.

Theoretically you can sprout millet, oats, rye and other grains. I have managed rye but not any of the others. Oats, unfortunately, are rarely, if at all, raw. Even when you buy oat groats you are getting a heat-treated product but you may be able to locate raw oat groats. Porridge oats are steamed. Again, such products are okay during the transition from cooked to raw food, but oats tend to produce a lot of mucus. Millet is raw but hulled and will not sprout. Even so, the variety of sprouts will provide you with years of happy experimenting!

Whole, raw oats, brown rice and barley won't sprout, but if soaked for long enough they will become valuable enzyme-rich foods which can be eaten raw and be a valuable and versatile addition to your raw food diet. Rice needs to be soaked for six days – change the water twice daily and rinse the grain well. Oats should be good in twelve to twenty-four hours (change the water and rinse twice in that time), though you may prefer them after thirty-six hours. Barley needs at least thirty-six, preferably forty-eight, hours in water. Change the water and rinse every twelve hours. Oat groats can also be ground in the grinder straight from the packet. You can then mix this flour with water and leave overnight or mix and eat straight away as a raw porridge. Add bananas, cinnamon, dates, raisins and other fruits. The oatmeal in shops has been steam processed to inactivate enzymes, so don't use it.

SEAWEEDS

A more politically correct term for seaweeds seems to be 'sea vegetables'. 'Weed' does sound a bit like an insult, though, of course, weeds make great food. Even Prince Charles likes nettle soup. I hope he likes sea vegetables, too, as they are very good for him. The benefits of seaweeds are discussed in detail in the chapter on diet and lifestyle. Here we'll concentrate on their taste.

Most people ought to start with an 'easy' seaweed, such as dulse or nori. Even if you never progress to any of the other ones and even if you manage to like only one type of seaweed, you'll be doing your body a great favour if you eat it every day. I must admit, whenever anyone professes to like seaweed they immediately go up in my estimation; it still seems to me to be a mark of an adventurous spirit to actually like the stuff, even though my whole family loves it so I ought to be used to it by now! And I've come across lots of children who very happily chomp their way through many sheets of nori, handfuls of dulse flakes and large strips of soaked kombu. So don't despair – if you like seaweed, you're not mad. They quite like it in Japan, too.

You can eat both nori and dulse straight from the packet (watch out for small shells when eating dulse), although dulse is pretty salty so I don't recommend too much of it, too often. Nori is great wrapped round vegetables, sprouts or chopped-up nuts and sauces. Roll it all up into a little roll and you have a very tasty snack. Divide the sheet into halves or quarters first.

My children love soaked kombu and they enjoy 'fishing' for the strips in the soaking vessel. If you leave it in the water too long it does develop a very fishy taste though. Try it after a few minutes – it should taste pleasant and it shouldn't be too tough for your teeth. Hijiki is another tasty sea vegetable that needs to be soaked but not too long. Overnight is too long. Try half an hour to an hour. When soaking, make sure all the pieces are well covered with water, otherwise you'll end up with some nasty, spiky surprises!

I have found that because of their strong character and distinctive taste, seaweeds do not mix well with certain other foods. When lentil sprouts, for instance, are mixed with hijiki, the sprouts take on some of the fishy taste and I don't enjoy that at all. In fact, hijiki just doesn't go in salads. Nor does kombu. But dulse (it's especially easy in flaked form – just sprinkle on to your salad), kelp powder and crumbled pieces of nori are divine. I often mix well-soaked brazils with finely chopped onion (finely chopped is lovely with dulse, bigger pieces of onion are nice in a huge salad. But not too big or the pleasure of eating will be lost and the whole affair might turn into an act of endurance and bravery instead!) and lots of dulse flakes for a quick snack. Or chop up the nuts and onion and put the whole lot, together with some avocado and dulse into a nori roll. You can add garlic, tomato, thin slices of courgette, slivers of red pepper, sunflower sprouts, chopped up shii-ta-ke or brown cap mushrooms and it tastes as good as 'normal' food while having the nutritional and rejuvenation potential light years away from that 'normal' meal. I hope you are beginning to see that the Gold Band programme (see Chapter Twelve), which uses only raw foods, supplements and herbs, is not the sacrifice you thought it would be. In fact, I enjoy my food far more now than I ever did when I could and did eat *anything*. And, of course, true Radical Rejuvenation is only really possible on a completely raw diet coupled with herbs and supplements and no animal products. As you have seen in the previous chapters, a raw diet is superior to a cooked diet. So the only thing standing in your way is habit. While I concede that habit can be a powerful force, you and your determination have much more power. And don't let any false starts deter you – every attempt at an all-raw diet will be making you healthier and stronger and younger-looking, so just keep it up.

FRUIT AND VEG

If you ate nothing else you could still manage to create an impressive and tasty diet from these food items alone. Together with RR supplements and herbs you would also be eating a diet of formidable rejuvenative power. I never tire of fruit. Let me remind you of what is waiting for you: papaya, avocado, mango, melon (water, honeydew, ogden, galia), pears, apples, oranges, bananas, tangerines, satsumas, lemons, custard apple, strawberries, raspberries, passion fruit, kiwi fruit, lychees, grapefruit (don't forget the pink one), sharon fruit, fresh dates, fresh figs, black grapes, white grapes, pomegranate. Then there are the red, yellow and orange bell pepper, tomato and cucumber, all strictly speaking 'fruit'. Even mushrooms are fruit in a sense, since they are the fruiting body of the fungus. And we haven't even started with the vegetables, which form a vast category of beneficial foods for humans. Just to remind you, here's a list of my favourite veggies which can be enjoyed in their raw state (have fun making you own list!): carrot, beetroot, sweet potato, courgette, Brussels sprouts, lettuce (cos, gem, Webbs and many others. Go for dark green rather than pale and wan as in iceberg – the colour holds the vitality factors), onion (especially the beautiful red onion – it is an exceptional source of quercetin, a bioflavonoid which protects your body against pollution and builds up your resistance to disease, particularly colds and flu and chest infections), garlic, broccoli, cabbage, spring greens, mizuna, daikon radish, radish, pumpkin, squash, spinach, red pepper and okra.

Before preparing your fruit and veg it is always best to wash them. Ideally leave the fruit and veg to soak for a little while in a bowl of water and vinegar (organic apple cider vinegar is perfect). This will wash off any horrible pesticides from the skin. I usually avoid peeling my fruit and vegetables, because many vitamins and minerals are found just under the skin.

Fresh herbs belong here too. Try and use some daily. Some of the nicest are basil, dill, thyme, chives, coriander, tarragon and even horseradish and chilli peppers. Be very careful with the seeds of the chilli pepper – *never* be tempted to eat them and try not to touch them with your fingers; the 'hotness factor' clings to them through numerous hand washings. Even hours later your fingers will retain the ability to make your eyes smart.

Just one word of explanation: as I've mentioned in the previous chapter, I don't use carob because it is sold roasted. Honey and dried fruit are very concentrated and can be hard on teeth. Most honey has been heated; and eaten soon after or before a meal containing meat or eggs it can lead to fermentation and terrible stomach upsets. For some reason, I have also seen this happen a few times when dried fruit was made into bars with spirulina. I suspect the spirulina was contaminated but do be very careful. I haven't come across this problem with chlorella. However, when the dried fruit is mixed with water and blended well, you can add other, fresh fruit and sweet vegetables without problem, though I would still keep away from spirulina in the mix. Free amino acid powder is perfectly fine.

You might wonder why fermented cheeses are okay if the fermentation caused by dried fruit is so bad. The answer is that fermented foods are all right during the initial stages of changing on to a raw food diet and they are all right if you find they agree with you. They do not cause the violent digestive upsets that dried fruit can cause or, more accurately perhaps, can facilitate – because you seem to need something such as meat or eggs for the fermentation to occur. The fermentation in these cheeses is more controlled. I suggest you try only the mild cheeses such as almond and see what you think. You could then try a cashew nut yogurt and if you don't develop mucus you could use the yogurt perhaps once or twice per week. Similarly, do not use fermented cheeses more than three times a week. These cautions do not apply to unfermented nut milks and spreads, dressings and butters. They are completely fine.

I also do not use ice cream. This is because I don't think it has any rejuvenative potential; it slows down digestion and the vitality of frozen foods is much lower than that of fresh foods, no matter what anyone says. You only have to compare a thawed-out strawberry with the article from the field to see that. Whether it's measurable in the laboratory or not, no one can persuade me that freezing doesn't destroy some of the vitality found in fresh foods. However, enzymes *do* retain their activity after freezing, so it's not that bad. I think dried fruit which has been frozen but is eaten at room temperature is much better than ice cream which has been frozen and is eaten cold.

I usually chop my salads by hand but I sometimes use a food processor when making vegetable loaves. Blenders and juicers, for some reason, do not seem to produce any detrimental effects. Illogical? Probably. But then I'm not sure that life is particularly logical. That's how we try to understand it, certainly, but logic isn't the only possible approach to reality and it may well not be the best. I'm even cautious in the use of electric nut grinders – if you've ever used one, you will have noticed the heat generated in the process. The nut mixture is actually quite hot immediately after grinding. Heat and oils (in the nut) are a bad combination, especially if you are choosing to eat for health, vitality and youthfulness. However, nuts can be *blended* in water in the blender jug and you can add any flavouring, such as avocados, carrots, spinach, mushrooms and onions for a raw soup or dried and fresh fruit for a sweet sauce or pudding. So you won't be missing out on the treats, that's for sure! And you won't be eating any free radicals with your meal. Another way to avoid heating up nuts and grains in the grinder is to fill it only half full. Much less heat is generated this way. And go for strong machines – they seem to have a better effect on the food, perhaps because they don't have to work so hard.

Now let's take a look at what is possible in the RR kitchen. I have arranged the recipes in the conventional way; Starters and Snacks, Soups, Main Meals, Sweets, Sauces and Dips, Drinks and a section on Fermented Foods as well as 'Recipes for Cheats' which you can choose to use if you wish. I find that this is the way I think about food, even though what I actually mean by Main Meal differs radically from what I used to mean. Sometimes I have grapes and it's a meal, sometimes they are more of a snack. However, rest assured you will not find 'a bowl of grapes' as an entry for a Main Meal. Though if you ever feel like making a meal of just a bunch of grapes, go ahead. Fruit makes delightful meals.

RECIPES

Please note: for recipes that use herbs and spices, add to taste where quantities are not specified.

Starters and Snacks

Everyone loves finger foods and small, tempting, tasty morsels. In fact, one of the most joyful discoveries to make about eating raw foods is that they all make such great nibbling food. What can be more tempting than a beautiful plate, decorated with slices of fresh mango, papaya, avocado, soaked almonds (they become delightfully sweet and fresh and crunchy after soaking. Leave them at least overnight, preferably twenty-four hours) and brazils, perhaps some pine kernels, round 'buttons' of banana, pineapple chunks and sliced apple. It really matters how you cut fruit, by the way. I know people who won't eat apple unless it has been cut into delicate rounds. Grated carrot is a completely different food from a whole one, an orange cut into quarters is more fun to eat than having to battle through all that skin and pith and end up with a soaked chin as well. So remember that often it's the *presentation* which can turn 'fruit' into a starter or 'vegetable' into a snack. Here are some more ideas to get you playing.

AVOCADO AND DULSE STARTER

One avocado   *Dulse flakes to taste*
Half an onion

Halve the avocado, remove the stone and cut the flesh lengthways into strips, then cut crossways. Don't cut through the skin. Remove the avocado pieces with a spoon using a scooping action. Chop the onion finely and mix with the avocado in a bowl. Sprinkle with dulse flakes. This recipe will serve one or two people as a starter or one person as a nourishing snack.

NORI ROLLS

Two sheets of untoasted nori   *Chopped onion, garlic and black*
Sunflower sprouts   *pepper*

Tear the nori sheets along the central fold, then halve and tear again, so that you end up with a quarter. Put to one side. Take one sheet and put a large spoonful of sunflower sprouts on the thin end near you. Spread them into an even line along the bottom. Add the onion, garlic and black pepper, then roll up into a roll, pressing slightly as you go to help shape it. Repeat with the remaining ingredients. You can substitute lettuce leaves for the nori if you wish. Spear the finished rolls with cocktail sticks if necessary, to keep them together. Add 'Yummy

Green Sauce' (page 201) to the sunflower sprouts at the beginning and continue as above for a delicious, filling snack. Wheat sprouts used instead of sunflower sprouts are delicious, too.

STUFFED TOMATOES

Four large tomatoes   *Chopped onion, garlic and black*
One small avocado   *pepper*

Wash the tomatoes and place on a large plate. With a sharp knife remove the tops from the tomatoes, then scoop out the middles with a spoon and place in a bowl. Add the flesh from the avocado, mash and mix well with the tomato flesh. Add the seasonings and stir well. Fill each tomato case with the avocado mixture and place a tomato 'hat' on top. Serve two tomatoes per person as a starter or a light snack meal.

MELLOW AVOCADO STARTER

One large avocado   *Two large, creamy bananas*

Halve and slice the avocado, remove the skin and chop into small pieces. Cut the bananas into chunky rounds. Mix the two kinds of fruit in a bowl. Serve. This recipe makes enough for two people.

STUFFED MUSHROOMS

Ten brown cap mushrooms or   *A teaspoon of fresh lemon juice*
*   large ordinary ones*   *One finely chopped onion*
Half a cup of pre-soaked pine   *Finely chopped fresh chives,*
*   kernels, drained*   *   parsley and basil*
Half a red pepper, chopped into   *Dried parsley*
*   small pieces*   *Black pepper*

Remove the stalks from the mushrooms, then wash and pat dry. Put the rest of the ingredients into the blender jug with a little fresh water and blend until smooth. To thicken the mixture if required, add roughly chopped cashew nuts to the blender. Spoon the mixture into the mushrooms and serve.

CREAMY MUSHROOM ROLLS

Four nori sheets
Sixteen brown cap mushrooms or
   eight shii-ta-ke ones
Half a cup of soaked almonds,
   drained
Quarter of a cup of soaked pine
   kernels, drained

A teaspoon of fresh lemon juice
Black pepper
Cumin powder
Dried parsley
Chilli powder
Finely chopped garlic and
   onion

Tear the sheets of nori along the central line and put to one side. Wash and dry the mushrooms. Place all the ingredients apart from the nori into the blender with a little fresh water to start the blending process. Blend until smooth. Thicken if necessary by adding chopped cashews to the mix and blend again. Place a spoonful on the narrow end of the nori sheet closest to you, dull side up. Make eight neat rolls.

CUCUMBER SANDWICHES

Half a cucumber, sliced into
   rings
One small avocado
One onion, sliced into rings

Black pepper
Dried parsley
Chilli powder (optional)
Cumin powder (optional)

Make the sandwiches by placing a slice of cucumber on the plate, spread it with the avocado 'butter' and top with an onion slice. Add the seasonings of your choice and decorate with dried parsley. Place a second slice of cucumber on top to complete the sandwich. Repeat until all the ingredients are used up – simple but delicious!

Soups

CREAM OF MUSHROOM SOUP

Half a cup of unsoaked cashew nuts

Ten brown cap mushrooms
or
Seven shii-ta-ke mushrooms

One teaspoon of fresh lemon juice

Black pepper

Blend the cashews in three cups of water. If you want to have a thick soup, use less water or more nuts; conversely for a thinner soup just use a little more water. Add the rest of the ingredients and blend until completely smooth. This soup may be chilled for an hour in the fridge. It will not keep well for long, however, as the cashews begin to ferment. You may choose to make a more yogurty soup by making a cashew nut yogurt first (page 206) and then adding the mushrooms and seasonings.

TOMATO SOUP

Ten tomatoes
A large spoonful of organic sultanas or raisins
Black pepper

Cumin powder
Dried parsley
Chilli (optional)

Chop the tomatoes into quarters and put into the blender. Begin to blend. Do *not* add water. You may need to stop every now and then to push the pieces of tomato closer to the blade and help the blender. Eventually there will be enough liquid produced from the tomatoes to whizz up all of them to a smooth, runny consistency. Add the rest of the ingredients and blend again until completely smooth. This soup is quite thick but you may thin it to the desired consistency with some water after you have blended all the other ingredients and completed the above process.

CUCUMBER SOUP

Half a cucumber
Two teaspoons of fresh lemon
   juice
Cumin powder

Black pepper
Chopped garlic
Chopped chives or chopped fresh
   parsley

Blend all the ingredients with two cups of water. Decorate with chopped chives or chopped fresh parsley.

Main Meals

When you're eating raw, main means salad. I live primarily on fruit, but my day isn't complete without a huge plateful of salad and even the little members of the family ask for it. The most favoured veggies in our house are onion, garlic, avocado, red pepper, tomato and cucumber. We find that carrot is nicest grated in salads; chopped carrot turns a meal into an ordeal, even if your teeth are perfect. Soaked sesame seeds make the salad into a complete, delicious meal. Seasonings and dressings are an art form. You can make a simple, elegant dressing from walnut oil, lemon juice and black pepper or a much richer concoction from soaked sunflower seeds, avocado, a little black pepper and water. We always sprinkle dulse over the finished salad before stirring everything together. Remember, the richer the dressing, the fewer the nuts or seeds should be in the salad itself. Take care to cut the vegetables into small pieces; they taste much better that way and are a lot easier to eat.

In our house salad is made in an enormous stainless steel bowl and by the time the meal is done, it's almost overflowing with goodies. And no one ever leaves any! That's because we're all real foodies. If you prepare your salads as described here, the RR way, you too will find them irresistible. And, by the way, nothing compares with salad as a filling, strength-giving food. It is the exact opposite of what is generally believed in the West, of course, but vegetables build really strong and healthy, vibrant bodies. Try it and see.

BASIC SALAD

*Half a cucumber chopped into
    slices and then cut into tiny
    pieces*
One large avocado, cut small
*Half a Webbs lettuce or a whole
    gem lettuce cut into small pieces*
Five tomatoes, chopped small
Five mushrooms

One large onion
Two cloves of garlic
One red pepper
*One cup of soaked sunflower
    seeds*
Black pepper
Dried parsley and cumin to taste
Walnut oil as required

Make sure all the vegetables are cut into small pieces. Some people
adore onions cut in circles rather than just chopped and garlic tastes
divine pressed in a garlic press, added to the walnut oil and mixed with
spices, then poured over the meal. Find out your favourite ways with
veg. Dill is also a lovely herb on salads.

AVOCADO AND TOMATO SALAD

One small avocado (per person)
Four tomatoes (per person)
*Basil, dry or fresh, finely
    chopped*

Garlic, finely chopped
*Walnut oil or extra virgin olive
    oil if it agrees with you*
Black pepper

Chop the avocado, or avocados if you are using more than one. The
best way to do this is to halve the fruit, take out the stone(s) and then
score lines vertically and then across the flesh, taking care not to cut
through the skin of the avocado. Then simply scoop out the chunks of
flesh on to a plate or into a bowl. Halve and then quarter the tomatoes
and mix gently with the avocado pieces. Season to taste. The
combination of avocado and tomato is really delicious. One of my
favourite meals!

MUSHROOM AND AVOCADO SALAD

One avocado (per person)   *Cumin, ground*
Six mushrooms of your choice   *Walnut oil (optional)*
(per person)

Simple but delicious. Prepare the avocado(s) as above. Wash or wipe
the mushrooms and chop them into small pieces. Toss with the cumin
and oil if you are using it. The cumin complements the taste of
mushrooms very well.

RAW OATMEAL PORRIDGE

One cup of hulled, raw oat groats   *Honey, ground pollen or raisins,*
Water   *whichever you wish, or a*
Cinnamon   *combination of all three*

There are two ways to prepare this porridge. You can either grind
the whole groats and add water, let them soak overnight and add
the cinnamon and your choice of sweetener, or you can soak the
whole groats and eat them in the morning, whole, with your chosen
additions. Actually, there are even more possibilities; you can grind
the whole oats in the morning with water and add sweeteners, you
can soak the whole groats with dried fruit and blend everything up
in the morning or you can even grind the oats, add water and
sweeteners and eat straight away! Whichever you choose, the result
is delicious and satisfying. By the way, strictly speaking, it's best to
soak the grain and even pour off the soaking water to remove
enzyme inhibitors and phytic acid, but in practice it doesn't really
matter.

VEGETABLE LOAF

Three large carrots
Chunk of cabbage
Four mushrooms
Three tomatoes
Black pepper
Curry powder

One small avocado
One cup of ground almonds
(make these yourself, don't use
the de-vitalised shop-bought
variety)

In a food processor (I don't often use this gadget because it is a bit rough on the vegetables, but every now and then it can add variety to your raw 'cooking') chop the carrots, cabbage, mushrooms and tomatoes until well blended. Add the spices, avocado and then the almonds. Turn out into a pie dish and press well. You should have a raw 'loaf' which can be sliced and placed on a plate. Add 'Yummy Green Sauce' (page 201) or the following, unfermented, 'cheese'.

UNFERMENTED 'CHEESE'

One cup of soaked sunflower
seeds
Three cloves of garlic
Half a teaspoon of vitamin C
powder

Parsley
Black pepper
Pinch of kelp powder or dulse
Water

Blend all the ingredients until smooth. You can make it runny and use as a sauce or thick to use as a dip.

WHEAT WITH MUSHROOM SAUCE

One cup of sprouted wheat berries
Chopped onion
One large avocado, chopped into
small pieces

Ten mushrooms
Half a cup of cashew nuts
Black pepper
Teaspoon of fresh lemon juice

Put the grain into a serving bowl. Stir in the onion and avocado pieces.

Blend the mushroom, cashews, black pepper and lemon juice with enough water to make a thick but pourable sauce. Result: yum!

COURGETTE, WHEAT AND CASHEW YOGURT SAVOURY

Four small courgettes
One cup of sprouted wheat
One cup of cashew nut yogurt

Quarter of a cucumber, thinly sliced
Black pepper

Cut the courgettes into thin slices and mix with the wheat berries in the serving bowl. Mix the yogurt with the cucumber and pepper and pour over the wheat and courgettes. This will easily serve two people or one very hungry one! You could decorate the top of the meal with some fresh, chopped herbs and small pieces of yellow, green or red peppers (red really are my favourite).

SPINACH AND SUNFLOWER SAVOURY

One cupful of spinach, chopped small
One cupful of sunflower sprouts, drained

Half a cupful of dulse flakes
Savoury walnut dressing

Place the spinach in the bottom of the serving bowl, cover with sunflower sprouts and dulse and pour the dressing on top.

SWEETCORN AND BARLEY COLD POT

Two sweetcorn cobs
Two cups of soaked barley, drained
Five tomatoes, washed and finely chopped
Half a cucumber, washed and finely chopped

One red pepper, washed and diced
One onion and three cloves of garlic, finely chopped
Black pepper
One tablespoonful of walnut oil (optional)

Remove the corn kernels from the cob. Place in a large serving bowl and mix thoroughly with the remaining ingredients. Serves two people.

PINK AVOCADO BOATS

Two large avocados

Half a teaspoon of fresh lemon juice

One red pepper, chopped

One thin slice of beetroot

Two cloves of garlic, chopped

Black pepper

Eight large lettuce leaves (any colour but the red ones are especially attractive)

Halve the avocados, remove the stones and scoop out the flesh. Keep the shells. Place in the blender (chop up the flesh roughly first to make the blending easier), blend until creamy, add the lemon juice and the red pepper and whizz until smooth. If necessary, add a little water to facilitate blending. When smooth, add the remaining ingredients, making sure everything has been well blended. Fill the empty avocado shells with the mixture. Serve on a bed of lettuce. Don't forget to eat the lettuce!

Sweets

My favourite 'pudding' is a creamy banana. There are so many delicious varieties of fruit, exotic and local, in the shops now that 'dessert' is probably the easiest part of raw eating. Exotic fruit salad, sliced fruit, segments, circles and triangles of fruit, pyramids and mounds of fruit, fruit in pretty, individual glass bowls, perhaps topped with a nut cream, fruit and nut 'milk' shakes, fruit layers topped with nut cream, topped with fruit layers, topped with nut cream. And you don't even have to feel guilty! Here are some very tasty ideas to get you into the mood and into the kitchen.

ROXY'S BEE BAR

Half a cup of pollen granules   *Raw honey*
Half a cup of almonds

Grind the pollen in a coffee grinder until it's fine, then add the almonds and grind again, processing both together and mixing them well. Use half of this mixture to cover a large plate and dribble well with honey. Add the rest of the mixture. Knead to form a pliant dough. If you need more honey add it until you've kneaded everything together. You can then pinch off pieces and roll into balls or form into bars. They will disappear as fast as you can make them!

ROXY'S BIG GEE BAR

Recipe as above for Roxy's Bee Bar but add one to two teaspoons of ground Korean ginseng for even more zing! Delicious, rejuvenating and energy-giving food.

MANGO AND BANANA DELIGHT

One large mango   *Freshly squeezed orange juice*
Two large bananas

Peel and slice the mango into small pieces. Cut the bananas into slices. Mix the fruit gently together and pour the fresh juice over it. Ruby-red oranges make a beautiful red, sweet juice.

DATE AND BANANA PIE

For the crust:
One cup of almonds   *Half a cup of dried dates or raisins*
For the filling:
Four bananas   *Half a cup of ground almonds*

Grind the almonds in a coffee grinder (experiment with other nuts and seeds; walnuts are nice and very nutritious, full of magnesium and high in protein, cashews are tasty, sunflower seeds are good and packed with power). In the food processor, process the dried fruit until it has formed a ball. Break up the ball a little with your fingers (be careful – switch off the machine if it hasn't got a safety feature), add the nuts and process again. Take out and knead this 'dough', then press into a pie dish. You could add pollen to the nuts sometimes if you wish. Make sure the whole pie dish bottom is well lined; if you can, extend the pie crust up the sides.

Blend the bananas in a blender (you may have to add a little water or fresh orange juice to start the process). Turn out into a mixing bowl. Add the almonds to thicken the whole mix. Use this to fill the pie crust. Decorate with slices of banana. Of course, this is just the beginning; try filling the pie crust with a mix based on Roxy's Bee Bar mixed with bananas, mangoes, fresh figs or strawberries! Remember that bananas and almonds (or other nuts) will thicken the mix.

BANANABERRY TRIFLE

Two large, creamy-ripe bananas
One teaspoonful of fresh lemon juice
Two cups of blueberries, blackberries, raspberries, strawberries, black grapes, whatever is in season

One cup of soaked brazils, drained
One cup of organic sultanas or raisins
Two large dollops of extra thick cashew nut cream (page 202)

Cut the bananas into chunky rounds, sprinkle with lemon juice, mix with the berries or halved grapes and arrange in two serving bowls. In the blender mix the brazils, sultanas or raisins and one cup of water until very smooth. Just before serving, decorate with extra thick cashew nut cream. This recipe makes enough for two people.

LYCHEES AND AVOCADO CREAM

One pound of lychees   *Two avocados*

Peel, stone and slice the lychees. Blend avocado flesh in a blender with just enough water to get the process going. Arrange the lychee pieces in a bowl or on a plate and pour the avocado cream over the sliced fruit.

Variations

You can substitute fresh, stoned, peeled and sliced dates, fresh, sliced figs, sliced mango or papaya for the lychees in the previous recipe and serve with avocado cream. Or make a head-spinningly delightful mixture of all the above before topping the whole lot with avocado cream. Heaven!

FRESH FIGS WITH CASHEW CREAM

Six fresh figs   *One cupful of runny cashew*
                                    nut cream (page 202)

Prepare the figs by washing and patting them dry gently. Remove their stalks. With a sharp knife, cut into quarters from top to bottom, leaving the segments attached at the bottom. Open up the fig 'flowers', three in the centre of each serving bowl. Pour the cashew cream on top, allowing a small, delectable lake of cream and fresh fig juice to form at the bottom.

ORANGE SEGMENTS WITH DATE SAUCE

Four medium-sized oranges,   *free-flow dates – they are*
   preferably seedless   *covered in mineral oil)*
Half a cup of stoned, dried dates   or
   (organic if possible. Don't use *One cup of fresh dates*

Peel the oranges, divide into segments, then slice the segments in half.

Blend the dates with enough water to make a smooth, fairly thick sauce (you will need to prepare the fresh dates by removing the stones, peeling if you wish and cutting roughly). Arrange the orange segments in a serving bowl (you have enough for two) and top with the date sauce.

MABEL'S TRIFLE

Two large bananas
Three dessert apples – red ones
   are nice
One pound of black grapes or
   white seedless, if you prefer

One cup of thick cashew nut
   cream (page 202)
One cup of pecan sauce
   (page 203)

Slice the bananas into thin rounds, divide into two lots and arrange in two bowls. Cover with a thick layer of cashew cream. Core and segment the apples, slice into chunks and divide between the two bowls, placing them carefully on the cashew cream layer. Halve the grapes and remove the seeds if you wish, top with more cashew cream. At the table, add pecan sauce. Eat immediately! By the way, 'Mabel' is my daughter's 'cooking' name – one of the world's most imaginative raw food cooks!

Sauces and Dips

CUCUMBER SAUCE

Half a cucumber, unpeeled
Four tomatoes
Almonds, soaked and peeled
   (about ten)

One garlic clove
Black pepper
A pinch of kelp powder

Chop the vegetables roughly. Blend the almonds with enough water to produce a 'milk', then add the vegetables, garlic and spices. Blend well.

YUMMY GREEN SAUCE

*One cup of soaked sunflower
    seeds*
Two cloves of garlic
Two teaspoons of curry powder
Juice of one lemon

*Two teaspoons of vitamin C
    powder*
Two small avocados
*Two handfuls of fresh spinach
    leaves, washed*

Blend the first five ingredients with enough water to make a thinnish cream. Add the flesh of the avocados, blend again. Add the spinach bit by bit and blend after each addition. You should have a lovely, tasty, green sauce. To thicken, add more avocado. Add parsley, fresh or dried, for extra taste. Delightful with a bowlful of sprouted sunflower seeds as a light meal or poured over a salad for something more substantial.

MABEL'S RED SAUCE

Four tomatoes
Three cloves of garlic
Two pickling onions
Half a small avocado
One red pepper
*One teaspoonful of fresh lemon
    or lime juice*

Black pepper
Fresh or dried parsley
Fresh mint
*Two large spoonfuls of walnut
    oil (optional)*

Wash and slice the tomatoes, peel and chop the garlic and the onions, cut the avocado flesh into small pieces, seed and cut the red pepper. Blend all the ingredients until smooth. Add just enough water to ensure that everything is blended very thoroughly. If you make the sauce quite thin by increasing the amount of water used during blending, you have a very tasty soup. The thick version makes a lovely sauce for a salad or a grain dish.

CASHEW NUT CREAM

Half a cup of cashews   *One cup of water*

Blend thoroughly in a blender at high speed. Use a little less water for a thick cream and about half and half cashews and water for extra thick cream. More water will give you a lovely pouring cream.

AVOCADO DRESSING

Two large avocados   *Three cloves of garlic, peeled and*
Juice from half a lemon   *chopped*
Half a green pepper, seeded and   *One onion, peeled and chopped*
   chopped   *Black pepper*
                                           Dried parsley

Blend all the ingredients together, with enough water to make a runny dressing. Wonderful with a simple green leaf salad made from: spinach, mizuna, Webbs and gem lettuces.

MUSHROOM DIP

Ten brown cap mushrooms   *One teaspoon of fresh lemon*
Two cloves of garlic   *juice*
Half a cup of cashews   *Black pepper*

Wash the mushrooms and pat dry. Slice. Peel and chop the garlic. Place all the ingredients in the blender with half a cup of water. This should blend up to a smooth, thick cream. Spread on celery sticks, use as a dip for carrot sticks or as a spread on lettuce leaves. Also nice as an accompaniment to a grain dish with a green salad.

PECAN SAUCE

Half a cup of dried dates (not *Half a cup of pecans*
free-flow)
or
Half a cup of raisins (organic if
possible)

Blend all the ingredients together with enough water to make a delicious sauce. For the pecans you can substitute soaked or unsoaked brazil nuts, almonds, walnuts, cashews, sesame seeds or sunflower seeds. If you add a banana you will have a creamier sauce. If you add a banana and an avocado you will have perfection!

Drinks

The best drinks are fresh, raw fruit and vegetable juices. Make them yourself and drink as soon as possible. Water is a problem because both tap water and bottled water can contain undesirable chemicals. The best bet is to drink distilled water although this solution is not perfect – distilled water doesn't taste good and it is, strictly speaking, cooked and dead. However, it does have *most* of the harmful chemicals removed (those with the same boiling point as water are retained), along with beneficial minerals (which should be abundant in your diet if you are eating a lot of raw foods though). Jug filters are better than nothing but make sure you replace them often. Too early is definitely better than too late. There are also other filters, more high powered than the simple jug filters, which can be plumbed into your water supply. These are also good, but, again, not perfect. Drink fruit juices as much as you can and consider investing in a distiller! But if you love bottled water, it's fine to drink it on occasion.

Since raw foods contain such a high percentage of water you will probably find that you don't get as thirsty as you used to. But, believe it or not, tea with milk was the thing I found hardest to give up! Now I don't even think about it. Rooibosh tea makes an excellent substitute for 'proper' tea, and, unlike the real stuff, is a pleasure to drink neat, as it were. Do be careful not to drink it really hot, though – hot liquids damage the delicate tissues of the digestive tract and destroy enzymes. I usually make my tea half-and-half with cold water. There are also delicious nut milks to make and enjoy. Try sesame seeds, cashews, sunflower seeds, almonds, pecans and brazil nuts. You may prefer to strain the milk after blending to remove the unblended particles. Nut milks improve in taste after an hour's refrigeration but don't keep them much longer than that. They make a great base for milk shakes; just add fresh fruit and a little dried fruit. For instance, banana, peach, raisins and cashew milk make a delicious drink which is good enough as a breakfast to see you through the whole morning without a single slump. Other possibilities are given below.

MELTED 'ICE-CREAM' MILK SHAKE

Twenty soaked, peeled almonds
Half a cup of dried dates (organic if possible)

A small piece of real vanilla pod (about quarter of an inch)

The name of this delicious drink comes from the fact that (we think) it tastes just like melted ice-cream. Pretty delicious! Blend the almonds first, using enough water to make a smooth 'milk'. Add the dates and blend again. Finally add the vanilla piece and blend very well. You could strain this but it's not necessary if you've blended it well. Yum!

BANANA BREAKFAST

Two bananas
A handful of Gou Qi Zi berries
Three spoonfuls of pollen, ground
Ground almonds (do this yourself)
Half a cup of dates (optional)
One spoonful of raw honey (optional)

One spoonful of royal jelly powder or *add a dose of your favourite royal jelly preparation*
One spoonful of white Korean ginseng powder (start with a teaspoon dose)

Blend everything together into one long, delicious, filling, rejuvenating drink! You can also add spirulina. Start with small doses – half a teaspoon or so. If you feel dizzy or unwell afterwards it means that the spirulina is cleaning you out too fast so decrease your next dose. Remember not to combine ginseng with coffee or vitamin C.

VEGETABLE BROTH

Half a cucumber   *Three tomatoes*
Three sticks of celery   *Fresh spinach (optional)*

Juice all the vegetables, stir, pour into a nice bowl and enjoy a healthy cup of soup like you've never had before.

MABEL'S APPLEGRAPPALADA

Three dessert apples, washed and   *One large bunch of grapes,*
cored   *preferably black*
Two cups of water

Blend all ingredients together. Strain. Drink. Yum!

CARROT JUICE

The Rolls-Royce of beverages. Czech researchers have found that carrots contain a substance similar to caffeine without the disadvantages. So remember carrot juice next time you crave your favourite form of caffeine, whether it is coffee, tea or chocolate. I have virtually lived on carrot juice at certain times in my life and I'm convinced it has aphrodisiac properties – it makes you feel good, anyway. I can only really recommend real, fresh, raw juice. Forget the bottles with shelf life.

Fermented Foods

These are useful in the changeover time from cooked to raw. I don't think they really build vitality. Try them and see what you think. I'd say they are fine for five or six months, then begin to use them less. In my experience they share many of the negative qualities of their dairy counterparts, including the ability to give you a blocked-up nose. They also share the positive aspects of dairy products – they taste delicious! Almond cheese in particular, fermented with crushed garlic, is a great favourite with everyone. The principle is the same whatever nut or seed you decide to use. Soak them overnight, rinse, blend with some fresh water and seasoning, pour into a container and let sit in a warm place for eight hours. Make the mixture runny for yogurt and thick and smooth for cheese. Here are two tasty ones to get you started.

CASHEW NUT YOGURT

One cup of cashew nuts   *Two cups of water*

Cashews should not be soaked beforehand. Simply whiz up the nuts with the water, pour into a clean, stainless steel, glass, pyrex or similar bowl, saucer or container and allow to stand undisturbed for eight hours. Cover with a clean tea towel to prevent things falling in. This yogurt is milk and sweet. If it tastes unpleasant, throw it out and start again.

ALMOND CHEESE

One cup of almonds   *Half a cup of water*
Three cloves of garlic, crushed

Soak the almonds overnight, rinse and blend with the garlic and water. Transfer to a clean container, cover with a clean tea towel and let it stand for eight hours. The cheese should have a pleasant, slightly sour taste. Just like cheese, in fact, but even nicer. Add black pepper, chopped chives, dried or fresh parsley, basil, cumin powder, chilli powder, onion pieces, even pineapple chunks (fresh and raw, of course).

* * *

The beauty of raw eating is that you can eat and prepare your food entirely to taste. Whatever you want to eat can make your next meal and there are no disasters. I have never experienced an inedible raw meal. Everything has a good taste because the ingredients are so good. The recipes and ideas given in this chapter are nowhere near exhaustive. They are for your inspiration and to provide you with a framework for your own, brilliant inventions – if 'Mabel' can do it so can you!

However, if you want to follow a less purist path here is the cheat's approach to Radical Rejuvenation. For these recipes you will sometimes need to use a cooker. So cheat with a little heat. But ssh! This is between you and me. I won't tell anyone if you don't. But seriously, Radical Rejuvenation is as flexible as you want it to be. For those unable to resist temptation here is the cheat's way:

Recipes for Cheats

EASY PEASY GOOD-FOR-YOU BREAD

As I recommend oil-free, marge-free, fat-free, sugar-free, salt-free bread, I'd better show you how it's done. Using vitamin C powder makes it so quick and easy it takes only about an hour from start to finish! The vitamin improves and speeds up rising wonderfully. And I don't ever spend much time kneading – I don't usually have the time and this bread doesn't mind at all. It comes out great every time. It really is very easy and here's how to do it:

Three cups of water
Two teaspoons of dried
  yeast

Half a teaspoon of vitamin C
  powder
Three pounds of wholemeal flour

Heat the water to lukewarm in a saucepan. In another saucepan mix the dried yeast and vitamin C powder (use either ascorbic acid powder from Boots or magnesium ascorbate, zinc ascorbate or potassium ascorbate powder if that's what you have – they will work just as well).

Add the water a little at a time to the yeast and vitamin C mixture, blending well to make a creamy liquid. Add all the water. In a large mixing bowl have the flour ready. Add the yeast and vitamin C liquid and mix well with the flour. You can use a wooden spatula for this step if you like. If the dough is too sticky add more flour, if it is dry and crumbly add more water (plain warm water will do if you have no more of the yeast mix left). Knead. You should have a nice, elastic dough pretty quickly. Form it into a ball, place in a large mixing bowl, cover with a clean tea towel and leave on top of the cooker or in a warm place. Light the oven, Gas Mark 8. The warmer the dough is, the better. Within reason – hot is not good. Warm and cosy is what you're after. If you are steaming something, the dough will love it. Leave the dough to sit for 10 minutes. After 10 minutes knead again and shape it into your loaf shape. Place in a floured tin, cover again and leave for 20 minutes in a warm place. After 20 minutes put the dough into the pre-heated oven for 30 minutes. Do not open the door for the first fifteen minutes to make sure the bread retains its risen shape. It is done if it makes a hollow sound when tapped. Let it sit for ten minutes at least to 'set' before cutting.

Hint: Adding ground walnuts to the flour (half a cup of ground nuts per loaf) will give you a truly irresistible loaf! You can also add garlic, onion or even sliced boiled potatoes (mix well with the flour before adding the yeast liquid). Eat this bread with Radical Rejuvenation salads.

VERY EASY TASTY PASTRY

This is wonderful made into biscuits, as a crust for pies, sweet or savoury, or as a case for pastries, bursting with delicious vegetables. Roll it into a long, thin roll cut into three and plait to make a pretzel-type biscuit. Sprinkle with extra sesame seeds for extra crunch. If you add a thick date or raisin purée to the dough you will have a lovely chewy biscuit. Here's what you need:

*One cup of sesame seeds (essential
   for crunch)*
*Half a cup of finely ground
   walnuts*

*One cup or more of wholemeal
   flour (same as for Easy Peasy
   Bread)*
Two cups of water

Mix the dry ingredients and make sure there are no lumps in the mixture. Slowly add the water. Knead. The consistency should be soft and pliable. Roll out and use as needed. The dough will keep in the fridge for two to three days and can be frozen, though I do not recommend freezing. Eating food which has previously been frozen will not give you the glow you seek. The quantity of dough from this recipe should be enough to cover the top and bottom of a medium-sized pie dish.

FILLINGS FOR TASTY PASTRY:

WOW APPLE PIE

Named by my daughter because that was the greeting this pie got the first time she tasted it (and all the times since).

*Two cups of raisins or
   sultanas or a mixture of
   the two*
*Half a cup of finely ground
   walnuts*
One cup of water

*Two pounds (or 1 kilo
   approximately) of cooking
   apples*
Cinnamon to taste
*One quantity of Tasty Pastry
   (previous recipe)*

Blend one cup of raisins and the ground walnuts with the water until it is very smooth but not too stiff. Add more water if the cream is too thick. Don't make it too runny, though. Chop the apples into small pieces (you don't need to peel them but do, of course, core them) and mix with the rest of the raisins/sultanas and the cinnamon. Line the pie dish with half of your rolled-out Tasty Pastry. Place a layer of apple and dried fruit and cinnamon on it and follow with a layer of the liquid mixture. Use half of the liquid mixture for this. Then add another layer of apple, raisin/sultana and cinnamon and finally top with the second half of the liquid mixture. Then place a layer of pastry on top. Make small slits along the sides and in the centre of the pie. If you have any pastry left over, make little flowers and decorate the pie. Bake at Gas Mark 8, for 20 to 30 minutes.

MADLY DELICIOUS DATE TREACLE TART

Half the quantity of Tasty Pastry
(just enough for the bottom
layer)
One cup of dates

Two to three cups of water
One cup of ground hazelnuts
Cinnamon

Prepare the pastry and line a pie dish. Bring the dates to the boil in a saucepan using two cups of the water given in this recipe. Simmer gently for 10–15 minutes. When soft and mushy, combine in the blender with the hazelnuts. Add the cinnamon. If the mixture is too thick and looks as if it might burn, add a little more water – you want it fairly thick, though; nice and gooey is just right. If the mixture is too runny, thicken it with some more ground hazelnuts. Bake at Gas Mark 8, for 15–20 minutes. Eat hot or cold. Cashew cream, either pouring or extra thick, is delectable with this tart! Good enough for parties.

SPREADS FOR BREADS

Sweet Spreads

These couldn't be easier or nicer – they are also raw! Simply soak some dried fruit of your choice in a bowl overnight (use only enough water to cover the fruit) and in the morning blend with enough ground nuts (hazelnuts and almonds are always a good and tasty choice) to form a thick, spreadable paste. Use it on toast, in sandwiches, as cake 'icing', pie filling or as topping for fruit salads. Some delicious combinations include: apricot and almond, date and walnut, raisin and hazelnut. Have a nice time finding your own favourite combinations.

Savoury Spreads

Red lentils are a neglected and very delicious food. Combined with a grain such as wheat they will provide you with complete protein and many vitamins and, minerals. It's also very easy to cook the lentils, then blend them and use the resulting purée as a sandwich spread. For flavour, cook the lentils with onion, garlic, black pepper, carrots, red peppers, shii-ta-ke mushrooms, seaweed or potatoes. Any or all of them. Then blend. The spread will thicken as it cools. You will be amazed how good it tastes.

So you see that cheating can still be very enjoyable even when it avoids health killers such as salt, sugar and oil. However, maximum radiance requires minimum cheating. And the *best* time for cheating is the morning – then your whole body has the rest of the day to regain its equilibrium.

CHAPTER TWELVE

Practical Programmes for Rejuvenation

Einstein said it was less than five. Some have gone as high as ten, some as low as one. They're talking about the percentage of brain power that you use. In other words, somewhere between ninety and ninety-nine per cent of your brain is untapped potential. So don't tell me you can't change your diet! Now that you've seen the reasons why you look old and see that you could use some changes, don't put the book down with a sigh. You don't have time for sighing – nobody does. But you have time for putting things right. Better than right, even. This chapter will teach you how.

First of all I will tell you something which you should recall whenever you feel despondent about any part of your rejuvenation programme. It is this: there has never been a better time for recharging your looks and health. I always get very depressed when people tell me things such as 'We were made to eat raw; just look at the animals, they all thrive on it'. I get depressed because, while it is true that animals thrive on raw food, we're talking about a very basic level of health and existence. In other words, I think 'Is that *all*?' That sort of instinctive health (which, by the way, is still much higher than the level 'enjoyed' or perhaps 'suffered' by the majority of people today) is not enough for me. I want BETTER. I want to live longer and look younger than cows and dogs and cats and tigers and orang-utans (all of which get old, grey and toothless if something doesn't eat them first). If you want it too, I've got great news for you: the programme described in this book makes it possible. *You* can do it.

In Part Two you learnt why RR works and read about some very convincing evidence for the supplements used in this programme, and the chapter on diet and lifestyle has provided ample evidence of the benefits of raw food eating. Most of this research is new and none of it was available before the twentieth century. In fact, some of the most harmful, but widely held beliefs regarding the role of diet and well-being, such as the myth that large quantities of animal protein are beneficial to humans, are a hangover from the less enlightened nineteenth century and have been refuted by modern research and modern clinical practice. Furthermore, you can go out and buy amino acids, enzymes, fatty acids, vitamins and minerals in supplemental form. This is a completely new development with huge implications for longevity and rejuvenation. I believe that a well-designed programme which makes use of the best supplements available can make an extraordinary difference even to the best raw food diet. And when such a programme is coupled with the herbs mentioned in this book, the effect on well-being and looks is phenomenal. Don't forget – many of the herbs are rare, valuable and were highly prized in the cultures which knew their potential. You can obtain them quite easily and all of them are cheap enough (apart from very high grades of ginseng, which are difficult to find and aren't strictly necessary, because for long-term use even average or good grade ginseng will produce good results) to use every day. Do not dismiss the herbs – they are a thousand times more powerful at producing rejuvenative effects than the best supplements. Many of their beneficial factors are yet to be discovered and some may never be. And none of them will ever be completely replicated by any laboratory anywhere. So go for the whole lot – diet, biological technology and the power of plants. Sounds like a lot of work? Then this chapter is for you!

Most people, even while looking for rejuvenation, even after reading the benefits of the RR Diet, aren't going to yell 'Yippee!' and rush their cooker to the nearest dump. (If you happen to be an exception, go ahead, you'll reap untold benefits!) So the question is, is it possible to experience Radical Rejuvenation *without* completely altering your diet and lifestyle? And, of course, the answer is yes. However, the more elements of RR you include in your life the faster and more spectacular the results will be. To help you in this process of change I have designed three programmes. They are called Basic, Intermediate and Gold Band and it is up to you which one you start with, although I would suggest that if you are new to many of the ideas and find the thought of changing your diet a bit too much of a challenge, then begin at the beginning, with the Basic, and stay with the Basic as long as you feel comfortable. RR is not a race. You will be improving your health and looks from day one as long as you implement the changes suggested, *however slowly* you do it. Your rate of ageing will decrease considerably whichever programme you decide to follow. So don't worry if you really can't face the rest of your life on rabbit food. The Basic and Intermediate programmes take this into account and therefore make great use of supplements and herbs. Again, don't worry – the cost is taken into account. This is not just for millionaires (though do try it if you happen to be one). All the products suggested are chosen for their Rejuvenation Power Value.

You will find that as you begin the programme there will be a tremendous improvement in your looks, well-being and even what is loosely termed as 'character'; with enough of the right sorts of nutrient, *everything* improves. Depending on how long you have been deficient in the basic building blocks of health, how low your cells are in enzymes, amino acids, vitamins, minerals and fatty acids, how much regeneration is needed, how badly your organs have been affected and how far 'ageing' has progressed, you will have to remain on your chosen programme for one to six months before you see some really good results. At that stage you can either progress to a higher level programme or remain with the one you are on. I do not suggest returning to your former way of eating unless you are yearning for a return to your former looks! Obviously, the most spectacular changes are reserved for those who progress to and remain on the Gold Band programme. If you go slowly through the Basic and then the Intermediate, spending at least three months at each level, you will find the process of change to the Gold Band almost painless! And, one day, you will suddenly find yourself anticipating a salad or a fruit meal with the same pleasure which you once only felt at the thought of a chocolate bar. And I speak as one who spent whole days eating chocolate. If you had asked me then about the purpose of life, I would have said it was chocolate and sex, in that order. I had to be *very* in love to even consider the possibility of sex first. I haven't eaten chocolate in years and now I don't even wish to. I'd rather have a nice, ripe avocado and banana platter which is my favourite meal. So let's look at how you can make Radical Rejuvenation work in your life. The best theory won't make you young. But the programmes given here will. All you have to do is follow them!

THE BASIC PROGRAMME

This one's for people who, for whatever reason, cannot go the Whole Way. Maybe the change to an all-raw diet is too much. Also this is a transitional programme. If you are used to a 'normal' diet the process of changing it, even for the better, can be a shock. This programme contains hints and supplements which will make such a change much easier and smoother. By the way, you can begin with any of the programmes; it isn't necessary to begin with the Basic. You can also use them in progression, spending as much time as you wish at each level. *And* you can always go back any time to the previous level.

I am assuming that you are eating a 'normal' diet right now. This means some junk food, some wholefood, perhaps wholemeal bread, some tinned food, cheese, yogurt, meat, fish, milk, tea, coffee, some alcohol, maybe cigarettes. Normal? I hope by now you can see why this is such a great recipe for OLD. But you're not one of those maniacs who is going to change it all *today*. Though that, too, is possible, just go to Gold Band. But if the thought of change gives you a tight stomach, relax. This is so easy you won't even notice it's good for you!

What You Need to Do

STEP ONE: AIM FOR HALF OF YOUR FOOD BEING RAW

The easiest way to do this is to begin each meal with a large salad, have fresh fruit for dessert and snacks, eat fresh fruit and soaked nuts for breakfast, perhaps accompanied by soaked oat groats, dried fruit and a nut or soya milk. You don't need to worry about calories or starch and protein combinations. When you eat a lot of your food raw, you begin to be able to digest your food efficiently, especially when your body is supported by liver-strengthening herbs (as it will be, on this programme and the subsequent ones) and enzymes which help your pancreas and your whole endocrine system. Nor do you need to worry about getting 'enough' protein. As we have seen, the problem for Westerners is *too much* protein. And you will be getting plenty of youth-building amino acids from the soaked nuts and from your supplemental doses of free form amino acids. Which brings us neatly to step two.

STEP TWO:
CUT DOWN *DRASTICALLY* ON ALL ANIMAL PRODUCTS

This means not more than once every two days. Okay – I know that if bread and cheese is your idea of heaven, this won't seem easy at first. But use all those spare brain cells! There's tofu, tahini, humous, tempeh, bean pâté, vegetable loaf, nut roast, cashew and mushroom pâté, olive pâté, avocado and onion sandwiches, avocado and tomato sandwiches, banana and peanut butter and celery sticks, fermented cheeses, cashew nut yogurt and milk, almond butter, nori rolls, raw cashew nut and mushroom soup, raw mushroom nut loaf and many more. You will find plenty of ideas to get you started in the chapter on recipes. You won't be hankering after that boring old cheese sandwich for long, I assure you. And you'll be looking and feeling better for it.

STEP THREE: CUT OUT ALL FRYING

If you want to look and feel young, you can't eat fried foods. Or any other processed or animal fats. This means no margarine (not even the new, non-hydrogenated kind – the oils used are still subjected to processing, hence damaging chemicals are produced. When they say 'soya oil' are they talking about genuine cold-pressed, unrefined, organic soya oil? No way, José!), no lard, no butter. *But* it also means: peanut butter (try to get organic, make sure it's aflatoxin tested and don't use it at every meal), tahini (again, go for organic if possible), raw, homemade almond, walnut, cashew or hazelnut butters. You could even dribble a little high-quality walnut or hazelnut oil on your bread or grains to moisten them. They do this sort of thing in Sicily using olive oil. Linseed, walnut or hazelnut oils are better because they supply you with the necessary Omega 3 fatty acids.

STEP FOUR: STOP SMOKING

Even if it takes you a whole year, start now. You just can't look your best if you are constantly feeding yourself free radicals. And if smoking 'helps you think' take Ginkgo Biloba. That *really* helps you think. And it protects your brain and liver against free radicals.

STEP FIVE: KEEP YOUR ALCOHOL INTAKE MINIMAL

Some alcohol is allowed on the Basic programme but it should really be an occasional affair, not an everyday habit. Try to buy organic wines – they are acquiring quite a reputation and you really don't want a cocktail of chemicals with your treat.

STEP SIX: CUT DOWN ON BREAD

Yes, even wholemeal. In fact, if you suffer from bloating or find it difficult to slim down, if you have painful varicose veins or haemorrhoids, or if you wake up feeling heavy and looking heavy, particularly around your eyes, you might be better off cutting bread out altogether. But cut it down, at any rate. Make it an occasional food – three times a week or so. Substitute rice pasta, 100 per cent buckwheat pasta and whole brown rice. If wholemeal pasta agrees with you, use that. If you notice any of the above symptoms, however mild, take heed. Either cut out all forms of wheat altogether or use it very occasionally.

STEP SEVEN: CUT OUT COFFEE AND TEA

Okay – try the *occasional* cup, if you must, but take an extra vitamin B complex on the days you do. Substitute Rooibosh tea for ordinary tea and one of the cereal coffees for coffee. Add soya milk, almond milk or cashew milk when the liquid has cooled a bit. Do not drink liquids while piping hot anyway; they kill enzymes fast!

STEP EIGHT: ADDITIONS TO YOUR DIET

Use sprouted seeds, soaked nuts, sprouted grains and pulses every day.

STEP NINE: ADD SEAWEED TO YOUR DIET

Aim for a daily dose of sea vegetables. You'll find the reasons for their importance in Chapters Ten and Eleven.

STEP TEN: CUT OUT SUGAR

You can't look great and eat this stuff. *However* if you do occasionally indulge, protect yourself a little – take an extra B complex capsule. See Chapter Ten for more about sugar. You may use dried fruit and raw honey instead. Don't cook with the honey. Dates make a very good sweetener for cakes.

Supplements for the Basic Programme

Where capsule quantities are suggested use that as a guide to quantities – always empty the contents, mix with water and throw the gelatin capsules away.

- *Pollen* – Take one teaspoon of pure, raw pollen every day. This will mend ageing skin, protect you against pollution, give you energy and improve your love life. Store the pollen in your fridge. You will find more information on pollen in Chapter Ten.
- *Spirulina, chlorella or Lake Klamath algae* – One teaspoon a day. Blue-green algae are great detoxifiers and beautifiers. To remind yourself of the reasons why they make such great anti-agers, turn to Chapter Ten.
- *Onion and garlic* – Eat a raw onion and three cloves of raw garlic daily. Red onions are good – they are rich in quercetin, a valuable bioflavonoid and free radical protector.
- *Seaweed* – Eat one sheet of untoasted nori and a handful of dulse each day.
- *Bioflavonoids* – Eat at least one of the following each day: a large bunch of black grapes, a handful of blackberries or blueberries, three oranges including the pith and some of the skin, a whole lemon with skin, a whole beetroot (without the skin!), three carrots.
- *Amino acids* – One teaspoon of Full Spectrum Amino Acid powder daily, or three to six capsules, will provide you with what you need.
- *Multivitamin/mineral* – One capsule daily. If you are under stress, or if you drink coffee or tea or alcohol, add a capsule of vitamin B complex.
- *Vitamin C* – Take 500 mg of this vitamin daily. If you have a powdered source, this means about a fifth of a teaspoon or

thereabouts. You can go as high as half or even a whole teaspoon if you are stressed, if you smoke or if you live or work in a polluted atmosphere. If you wish to cut down from a high dose, always do it gently – take at least four days, preferably a whole week of gradual reductions in the dose before you reach your lower target. For instance, if you have been taking a whole teaspoon of powder (three grams) to help you deal with an illness, hay fever or stress at work and now wish to return to your maintenance dose of 500 mg (half a gram), begin by cutting down 500 mg on the first day and continue in this way until you are back on 500 mg.

- *Vitamin E* – Take 200 i.u. as a maintenance dose. On top of this, add 1000 i.u. to each 250 ml of walnut (or other) oil you use for salads or as a supplement.
- *Beta carotene* – Take 7500 i.u. each day. Double this if you are suffering from a respiratory disorder or if you have a cold, if you smoke or if you live or work in an area high in airborne pollution.
- *Enzymes* – Take three capsules of Spectrumzyme or another multi-enzyme supplement with each meal. Take it at the *beginning* of your meal, that way your pancreas gains the maximum benefit.

    You almost don't have to change your diet if you add lots of enzymes to your daily diet. Isn't that good to know! You know I wouldn't tell you to eat real junk but enzymes will go a long way to sorting out the occasional foray into Plastic Food Land. Three Spectrumzymes are all you need for a basic tone-up. Enzymes help you to achieve great muscle tone and lose weight, as we saw in Chapter Five. Exogenous enzyme supplements such as Spectrumzyme greatly reduce the load on the pancreas, increase thyroid function and help you to lose weight. How much you stimulate this process depends on the amounts of enzymes in your diet. This is why I suggest that everyone takes enzyme supplements, even those following a completely raw food diet.

- *Magnesium and calcium* – Take one capsule daily. It should provide twice as much magnesium and calcium.

- *Organic Sulphur* – Three capsules daily for thicker hair, smoother skin and protection from pollution. Turn to the chapter on minerals if you want to find out more.
- *Histidine or Catuaba* – or both! For great sex and *real* rejuvenation, don't leave this one out. Take histidine on an empty stomach with half a capsule of B complex (giving you 25 mg of the major B vitamins) and one capsule of magnesium (providing 100 mg of elemental magnesium) at least half an hour before breakfast. Add the contents of two Catuaba capsules (a minimum dose – double it if you like) to your breakfast regime.
- *Echinacea* – Half a teaspoon of tincture each day. You can use *Echinacea angustifolia* or *Echinacea purpurea*. Both species of this marvellous herb will enhance immune function.
- *Essential fatty acids* – One to four large spoonfuls of walnut oil or linseed oil. See the chapter on EFAs for a detailed discussion of EFA supplementation. Also take half a teaspoon or two to four capsules of evening primrose oil daily.
- *Gou Qi Zi* – Eat one handful of the berries every day. The best way is to add them to a fruit mix. There are some ideas in the recipe chapter to get you started.

This is the Basic maintenance programme. All of the supplements can be taken with breakfast or some other meal of your choice (though if you take them with supper you will almost certainly feel too lively to sleep – not necessarily a disadvantage!) with the exception of enzymes, which should be taken with every meal, and histidine, which should not be taken with a meal at all.

You may, of course, add as many other supplements as you like, especially herbs and herbal anti-oxidants. These hold an essential key to effective, visible rejuvenation.

Externals for the Basic Programme

- Cut down on detergent-based soaps and shampoos. You will help your skin, hair, the rivers, fish, wildlife and your finances! Alternatives are discussed in the chapter on diet and lifestyle.

- Use VitaSorb C on your face daily. Night-time is the best time for this. Protect your clothing – VitaSorb is yellow.
- Use enzymes on your face. Every morning improve your skin with a quick enzyme treat. It is described in detail in the chapter on skin rejuvenation.
- Include some EFAs in your skin care regime. This is simple. Just apply some walnut, hazelnut or linseed oil to your face before you brush your teeth at night, wait till it has been absorbed a bit while you finish your teeth, then add VitaSorb C and you're done.
- Always use a sunscreen. I must admit that I don't *always*. B vitamins, no sugar and beta carotene will go a long way in protecting your face from burning. Also propolis cream has been found to repair and prevent sun damage when applied to exposed skin. Plus sulphur, vitamins E and C and a little selenium in your multivitamin/mineral. But do add a sun filter, too, as often as you can!
- Face Aerobics and Movement Therapy for the hair. At the beginning, once a day is almost a must. Though Face Aerobics can be time-consuming, they're worth being strict about. As you improve, you may be able to relax a bit. The hair treatment is quick and easy – just do it before you brush your hair in the morning.
- Cold baths. If you can bear this, do it. It's very beneficial but it can be *difficult* to begin the day with the cold splash. So this one is optional.

THE INTERMEDIATE PROGRAMME

The stakes are *much* higher on this one. With the Intermediate programme we come to a whole new level of possibilities. It's faster, deeper and quicker. The results are more *visible*. If you don't have too many vices to overcome and if your veins are filled with adventure as well as haemoglobin, don't tie yourself up in the Basic – begin right here! More is required of you but you stand to gain more, too. The changes are mostly in the diet, as you would expect if you've been paying attention. The more raw you eat the younger you look; the more cooked you eat, the older you look. But I always advise the use of herbs and supplements as well because that way you get superb results, not just great. And that's why this is called *Radical* Rejuvenation.

What You Need to Do

You follow all the recommendations for the Basic programme but this is a higher league – where it says 'maybe' in Basic, read 'no' for Intermediate. This means no coffee, no sugar, no bread, no animal products, definitely no cigarettes, no margarine and *very* close to no alcohol. This is not as high as you can go yet, so a little tipple every now and then (on the best organic stuff you can find) is allowed. As is a chocolate cake when it's your birthday, although you ought to look at the great and undeniable delights of exotic fruit salads.

But the great changes are in what you *can* eat on this programme. With the change in the Rejuvenation Quotient comes a little quantum leap. We hop from fifty per cent of your food raw to seventy-five or even ninety per cent. You decide. If you feel strong and young and energetic, go for ninety! You might even try the occasional all-raw day. Here we are in Serious Rejuvenation Land, especially if you add the following rejuvenators to the supplements mentioned in the section on the Basic.

On top of the Basic Supplements take these. You may add these to your Basic programme, too, if you wish.

• *Milk thistle* – Liver protector par excellence. Take one teaspoon of the powdered seed or two to four capsules containing the powdered herb. Do not take this herb in tincture form unless it is a genuine one-to-one herbal extract – you'll be able to tell by the price. Extracts are very expensive. They are also much darker than tincture. The active components of this herb are not easily extracted in alcohol. My advice is to take the powdered herb. Stir the powder into a cup of water or fresh juice at breakfast. It has a rather nice taste, which is unusual in such a powerful liver tonic. Liver tonics are usually bitter.

- *Astragalus* – One teaspoon of tincture daily or one teaspoon of the powdered root.
- *Chaparral* – One of the most powerful anti-oxidants anywhere. Take it for that reason because you certainly won't be taking it for its taste. *Very* bitter. But it gets easier – soon you'll be drinking it down without so much as a blink (and pigs will fly). Still, it's *really* good for you, so take some. Ten drops of the tincture each morning is a good start. Take it on an empty stomach just before breakfast. Increase the dose to half a teaspoon if you can!

As you start refining your diet and eating more raw food, you may notice that certain foods which you could eat without a problem until recently, including the heavier raw foods such as fermented cheeses, soaked nuts and certainly many of the cooked foods, are beginning to sit heavily in your stomach and make you feel less than vibrant when you wake up in the morning. This is a natural progression and indicates that your system is in much better running order. Remember those silted up basement membranes? They're going and in their place you're getting clean membranes and better intercellular transport. Which means that you need less food to nourish your body more fully than ever before. It means your body is beginning to function just like a younger body!

We all know people who insist that they can eat *any*thing and never put on weight or get ill. Well, part of the explanation for that is that their bodies are so silted up by toxins that even the toxins can't get through. But they don't get out without causing havoc, that's for sure. Also, most people who say they're never ill rarely mean exactly that. Often they exhibit quite serious symptoms of imbalance, such as stiff backs and joints, but they put that down to 'age'. You know by now what everyone ought to know; 'age' is cell malfunction and there are ways to slow it down, avoid it and reverse it. Awareness is a big part of the process. If your body tells you thàt what you're feeding it hurts, *listen*. Rejuvenation is not static and it isn't maths. Rejuvenation is an alive process. There will be surprises. You will find that you no longer desire certain foods that previously had a hold over you. Conversely, you will develop cravings for foods which you previously found unattractive – even seaweed! I have noticed that the more raw food people eat, the more they enjoy it. I know it sounds silly but it isn't. A meat eater doesn't enjoy fruit and vegetables nearly as much as a vegan, for instance. It wasn't until I began to eat all my food raw, years ago, that I first experienced the pleasure of a whole plateful of mizuna greens with olive oil and garlic dressing.

Externals for the Intermediate Programme

On the Intermediate programme you are entering an interesting stage – the more you do internally, the less you need to do externally. If you do yoga you'll find that your body remains flexible even after a gap in your practice sessions. Your skin will look good even first thing in the morning. Continue with the externals, however, especially with VitaSorb C and linseed or walnut oil, plus ten drops of an essential oil in 50 ml of a carrier oil such as linseed or walnut. You could try doing Face Aerobics less frequently – four good workouts a week should be sufficient. Movement Therapy for hair doesn't take long – do it every morning before you brush your hair. Also continue with the daily cold baths. If you are doing them, that is! They are worth it, but I understand that they are not everyone's favourite way to begin the day. Though, actually, the worst part is *thinking* about it. Once you're in, it's exhilarating!

The best way to take herbs, and the easiest, is to mix tinctures together in a clean bottle and mix a teaspoon of each mix in the morning in some water. Here is an effective mix for the Intermediate level which can be used at any level from Basic to Gold Band. Even people who haven't made any alterations in their diets have gained great benefits from taking these herbs.

TINCTURE MIX

In a clean bottle mix:

One part Echinacea   *Half part chaparral*
One part Astragalus   *Half part ginger*
One part He Shou Wu

Shake well. Take one teaspoon daily. You may increase the dose to twice or even three times daily if you are under stress of any sort.

By the way, measurements using 'parts' are an easy way of putting together herbal prescriptions. A 'part' can be anything, a teaspoon or a cup, depending on the size of your container and how much mixture you wish to make. Just remember to keep to the same size 'part' throughout the recipe. Powdered herbs can also be mixed in this manner and you will find a recipe for a powdered mix in the Gold Band programme. Mixtures like these make herb taking very easy – you just take a teaspoon or two of the mix, stir it into some water, drink and that's it!

THE GOLD BAND PROGRAMME

Just in case you thought this one's for saints, let me tell you that aphrodisiacs feature heavily in the Gold Band programme. It is most certainly not about hair shirts and self-denial. In fact, you can omit most of the demanding practices from the Basic programme, such as Face Aerobics and cold baths, and still look better than you ever did before.

What You Need to Do

Do not omit any supplements from the Basic and Intermediate programmes. Add the following herbs:

- *Muira Puama* – This goes well with Catuaba, another aphrodisiac.

Take one teaspoon of the mixture (mix them half and half if you have both the herbs in powdered form) or half to one teaspoon of Muira Puama alone.

VITALITY HERB MIX

This combination of powdered herbs is very effective at strengthening your body against illness and daily use will make a visible and beneficial difference to your hair and skin, your nails and bones and your vitality within weeks.

This is what you need:

Three parts powdered He Shou Wu
Two parts powdered Astragalus
One part powdered Ginkgo Biloba
One part powdered alfalfa herb
Two parts powdered Schizandra
One part powdered nettle
One part powdered ginger
One part powdered Gotu Kola
One part powdered milk thistle
Half part powdered horsetail
Two parts powdered rosehip shell
Two parts powdered spirulina
* Two parts powdered Catuaba
* Two parts powdered Muira Puama

Mix the powdered herbs well in a large container and keep in a cool dry place. Take one to three teaspoons daily in water. (* These two herbs may be taken by themselves if you wish to take a larger dose, as suggested above.)

Gold Band means raw. You may, of course, incorporate the Gold Band supplements into your life no matter what you're eating, but Gold Band rejuvenation depends completely on raw food as well as supplements. Without 100 per cent raw you don't get Gold Band. Without the supplements and herbs, ditto. You need the whole lot. If you have pure adventure with no room for haemoglobin running through your veins, start with this programme. Otherwise work up to it at your own speed. At this level you will be guided very strongly by the true needs of your body – you can't cheat even if you wanted to. And your food is getting lighter and includes more and more fruit and less of the heavier, fermented sprouted foods. You may find you hardly ever need them at all. Soaked nuts may still be fine occasionally, as will veggies, especially the fruit-type veg such as tomatoes, cucumber and avocados, but carrots and beetroot are also good. Your body will let you know. Most people find that they no longer need oil supplements – in fact, they seem to become detrimental to many people at this level, causing stiff joints and a heavy body. On the other hand, herbs are *essential*. Also, seaweed ought to be on the menu at least once a day. Fresh, raw juices are delightful and always essential.

Gold Band means pretty much perfection, even if your fruit and veg aren't all organic. Your body is getting daily doses of active enzymes, vitamins and minerals in their most biologically active forms, easily assimilable amino acids, bioflavonoids and lots of goodies that science has not yet even discovered. I hope you all graduate or even start with Gold Band as soon as you can. You could have a Gold Band weekend, fortnight or month whenever you felt in need of extra vitality, even if you didn't feel able to stay on it forever. And, don't forget, the Gold Band herb mix is for everyone, even those who choose not to change their diet one little bit.

Gold Band Externals

Although you'll be looking great and feeling fantastic pretty much all the time, you still need some external care if:

(a) you have sunbathed extensively in the past and
(b) you live in a polluted area.

Which means all of us, one way or another. So use a sunscreen, linseed or walnut oil, evening primrose oil or any other treatments from the chapter on skin rejuvenation which appeal to you. VitaSorb

A, VitaSorb E or VitaSorb C should always be included, too. A sunscreen gives your skin added care. Although Face Aerobics and cold baths are not strictly necessary at this level, I wouldn't give them up, especially the face exercises.

Easy really, isn't it?

I hope that you will experience the possibilities of Radical Rejuvenation for yourself and that you will enjoy the process. I hope that you, too, will find out that your body is capable of miraculous regeneration and great health and well-being. And I hope that you will find out what I have found to be true – that age is nothing to be afraid of.

HOW TO CHEAT AT RADICAL REJUVENATION

OK, OK, I know – *what is there to live for?* So you can have a great body that moves like it was made to move and a face that looks years younger than you, you can be sexy and firm and vital and vibrant but can you really never eat anything that wouldn't make a rabbit smile? Is an all-raw diet the only way to youthfulness and is it *forever*??

The answer is yes and no. Yes because only an all-raw diet will make you look and feel the best you can ever be. And no because we're talking Real Life here. So here's how to cheat on Radical Rejuvenation *and* still look better, miles better than you've done for a long, long time.

The Cheat's Programme
CHECK LIST

- Always start each meal with something raw even if it's just an apple, a carrot stick or a glass of freshly squeezed orange juice. A good deal of damage caused by cooked foods is avoided by this single, simple step.
- Follow this with grains and vegetables. Make these the bulk of

your cooked foods. Supplement generously with pulses and *lots* of raw fruit and vegetables and you have a VHD, Very Healthy Diet. To make it into a VRD, Very Rejuvenating Diet, keep increasing the percentage of raw veg and fruit and never let it fall below fifty per cent of your food intake. Eighty is even better.

- Next, no animal products. On good days, OK? Every time you eat animal products you make yourself look older. But if you do indulge just make sure you have a nearly all-raw day the day after. And plenty of fresh fruit and vegetable juices (not bottled). Protect your body further by adding two extra drops of VitaSorb A to your diet on the day (equivalent to 500 i.u.) and a teaspoonful of sarsaparilla or golden seal tincture. These measures mop up the toxins created when you eat animal proteins. Don't use vitamin A, sarsaparilla or golden seal if you are pregnant or lactating. For spreads, use raw nut butters wherever possible. Organic (raw if possible) unsalted butter is better than margarine. Margarine has more in common with plastic than food!

- Chocolate, junk food, coffee and other nasty habits. Are you kidding? But then, you're a self-confessed cheat so of course you're going to have some. OK. Follow it with as much raw food as you can manage for at least one day and double your intake of B complex vitamins and liver tonics on Cheat Days. I am not a fan of anything that comes pre-packed from a factory, whether it's soya milk or chocolate and if you want to look really good, learn to stay away.

- Before settling into the Radical Rejuvenation style which suits you best you could try this programme for six months: two months on the Basic, two months on Intermediate and two months on all-raw Gold Band or at least fifty to eighty per cent raw. This will get your body sufficiently clear for you to begin to feel and see the effects that different foods produce on your looks and well-being. After this initial six months you should be in a pretty strong position – aware of your body and its responses, your addictions and cravings less strong. Then you can decide on the approach that suits you and your lifestyle best.

- If you're a Cheat, don't neglect your supplements and herbs. This will help your body enormously to deal with any undesirable effects of your indulgences.
- If you really *love* tea switch to green tea which has been shown to contain anti-cancer compounds.
- No frying. Well ... Butter, olive oil or sesame oil are best if you really have to fry. Keep it short and sweet and don't go for smoking point. Use as little oil as possible. Leave a little moisture on the food before frying to help reduce the amount of oil absorbed. Keep frying down to almost non-existent. Steaming, poaching, grilling and baking have great potential. Get to know it!
- The use of oils. Expressed oils can contain harmful cis- and trans-fatty acids and produce free radicals in the body. But eating salads and steamed veg without some kind of an oil dressing is an art not easily acquired (though it *is* possible). Refer to the chapter on essential fatty acids for the best choices of oils. Get to love chilli. Make salads with avocado in every mouthful. Make dressings with nuts and seeds and lemon and garlic. And if all that fails, use the very best oils you can find and treat them with care. Keep them in your fridge and don't leave them in the light for any longer than you have to. Put the caps on as soon as possible.
  Hint: User-friendly salads are cut small with all rough parts removed – when well-mixed the avocado spreads itself around like the heat in the Caribbean and you might well find you actually come to prefer salads without oil by doing it this way!
- Nuts and seeds. It's true that they contain enzyme inhibitors but having to soak them each time can be a pain as well as limiting the choice of the nuts you can eat and how you use them. Cashews, for example, are not very nice soaked. Personally, nuts and seeds don't suit me, whether they have been soaked or not. My husband, however, thrives on soaked brazils and even does quite well on unsoaked ones. So if you fancy a handful of almonds or cashews or pecans and even some dried fruit (which should normally be severely restricted because it is very sweet, not exactly raw and harbours a wide range of potentially nasty

microorganisms) try them and see. If you look and feel a bit heavy the following morning at least you will have learnt something about your body's needs. My guess is that most people first embarking on raw foods will find nuts to be an acceptable and tasty food. The body is already used to a certain amount of heavy, dense foods from the 'normal' diet. If you get indigestion after nuts, eat them soaked. Throw away the rinsing water as it contains the enzyme inhibitors.

I hope that by now you can see that Radical Rejuvenation is for everyone. Even if you are in love with chocolate and chips the simple addition of raw foods can begin to swing your biochemistry to aliveness and vitality. You are not expected to jump straight in and eat nothing but raw foods forever starting now! Far from it. I know very well that changing your diet, especially to raw foods which are so much lighter than the foods we normally eat and therefore, at first, less satisfying and comforting, will take time. The information in this book is here to help you make the right choices for your looks and well-being even if it takes you several months or even years to accomplish your goal. The truth is, however, that the very simple changes described in this book and, especially, a diet composed entirely of raw foods with no animal products can produce a remarkable reversal of the changes we call 'ageing'. Even just getting close to the ideal, or getting as close as you can at any given time, will show you some of what is possible.

Radical Rejuvenation is an exciting adventure. Each one of you will embark on your own personal journey into looking and feeling younger. Try it. Remember that once you get on board you will be leaving the fear and the 'look' of old age behind for good. Bon voyage and all the best. Get ready to wave goodbye to sags, bags, wrinkles, a non-existent sex life, a tired body and a tired mind and get ready to welcome a new and younger you.

Sources

UK

Organic Sulphur, Full Spectrum Amino acids, VitaSorb C, VitaSorb E and all other BioCare and BioScience products can be obtained from the Nutri Centre either directly or by mail order:

The Nutri Centre
7 Park Crescent
London W1N 3HE
Tel: 0171 436 5122 Fax: 0171 436 5171

CC raw pollen, chlorella, organic linseed and organic linseed oil are available by mail order from:

Advanced Nutrition Ltd
8 Chilston Road
Tunbridge Wells
Kent TN4 9LT
Tel: 01892 515 927

Spirulina is available from:

Xynergy
Ash House
Stedham
Midhurst
West Sussex GU29 0PT
Tel: 01730 813 642 Fax: 01730 815 109

B complex, multivitamin and mineral, potassium ascorbate, magnesium ascorbate, VitaSorb C, VitaSorb E, Spectrumzyme, Derma C, beta carotene, GLA, linseed oil in capsules, Organic Selenium and much more can be obtained mail order from:

BioCare Ltd
Lakeside
180 Lifford Lane
Kings Norton
Birmingham B30 3NT
Tel: 0121 433 3727 Fax: 0121 459 4167

They will mail order to just about anywhere in the world. Add 15 per cent to the prices for this.

Eastern herbs in powder, cut or tincture form and many Western herbs in tincture form can be obtained from:

East-West Herbs
Langston Priory Mews
Kingham
Oxfordshire OX7 6UP
Tel: 01608 658 862 Fax: 01608 658 816

Minimum amounts are half kg or half litre.

Eastern and Western herbs in powder, cut or tincture forms, also pollen, propolis, royal jelly and spirulina powder, Pau D'Arco, Muira Puama and, in the near future, Ayurvedic and Brazilian herbs can be obtained by mail order from:

The Herbal Apothecary
103 High Street
Syston
Leicester LE7 1GQ
Tel: 0116 260 2690 Fax: 0116 260 2757

Minimum amounts are half kg or half litre but they can advise you if you wish to purchase smaller amounts.

Brazilian herbs and *Rosa mosqueta* oil are available by mail order from:

Rio Trading Company (Health) Ltd
Rio House
2 Eaton Place
Brighton

East Sussex BN2 1EH
Tel: 01273 570 987 Fax: 01273 691 226

Suppliers of good herbal products:
  Gerard House Ltd
  475 Capability Green
  Luton
  Bedfordshire LU1 3LU

  Potters Herbal Supplies
  Leyland Mill Lane
  Wigan
  Lancashire WN1 2SB

  Baldwin & Co
  171–173 Walworth Road
  London SE17 1RW
  Tel: 0171 703 5550
They will supply small quantities of herbs and tinctures.

  Mayway Herbal Emporium
  34 Greek Street
  London W1V 5LN
For Eastern herbs.

AUSTRALIA

This company will export herbs all over Australia. One of the best
companies in the world, dealing with herbs of superb quality (reflected
in the price):
  MediHerb PTY Ltd
  PO Box 713
  Warwick
  Queensland 4370
  Tel: 00 61 7661 4900

CANADA
Gaia Garden Herbal Apothecary
2672 West Broadway
Vancouver V6K 264
Tel: 00 1 604 734 4372 Fax: 00 1 604 734 4376

USA
Perhaps the best in the USA:
  Blessed Herbs
  109 Barre Plains Road
  Oakham
  Massachusetts 01068
  Tel: 00 1 508 882 3839

  Lotus Light
  1008 Lotus Drive
  Silverlake
  Wisconsin 53170
  Tel: 00 1 414 889 8501

  Four Seasons Herb Co
  17 Buccaneer Street
  Marina Del Rey
  California 90292
Sells Chinese herbs and herb products by mail.

  BioScience
  2398 Alaska Ave
  Port Orchard
  Washington 98366-8214
  Tel: 00 1 360 871 1234 Fax: 00 1 360 871 6178

Index